What People Are Saying About . . .

The Financial Wisdom of Ebenezer Scrooge

"This book deserves wide readership among those seeking to understand our often tangled and always impactful money relationships. Carry this book with you as a wise and trustworthy guide on your journey to healing, harmony, and happiness around money."

Edward A. Jacobson, Ph.D.
Psychologist, Coach and Consultant

"This book is designed to help the reader go into the muddy waters of family teachings, emotional controls and unresolved conflicts in order to free the reader from the painful problems around money."

Sharon Wegscheider-Cruse
Co-Founder of the National Association
of Children of Alcoholics

"This insightful book is worth its weight in high-yield bonds."

Suzy Farbman
Author of *Back from Betrayal: Saving a
Marriage, a Family, a Life*

"*The Financial Wisdom of Ebenezer Scrooge* is one giant step beyond the financial self-help books you'll find on the shelf of your local bookstore. While other books simply increase your knowledge about financial issues, this one helps you change the persistent behavior patterns around money that block your path to success. Better yet, by hooking the lessons to a story that we all recognize, it makes these transitions easy to relate to."

Bob Veres
Consultant/Lecturer to the Financial Planning Industry
Recently named one of the twenty-five
most influential people in the Financial Planning industry.

"Like a lot of people, I guess, money is something I have big worries about. This fine book is straightforward, direct and readable. It reflects professional knowledge and is quite different than other books about money. Most of all, it is useful; that is, it works!"

Alvin R. Mahrer, Ph.D.
Author of *The Complete Guide to Experiential Psychotherapy*

"This is one of those books that should be on an essential reading list for high school students."

David Lechuga, Ph.D.
Director, Neurobehavioral Clinic and Counseling Center
2005 President of the California Psychological Association

"These insightful authors deliver an incredibly potent, step-by-step formula for creating limitless wealth out of any individual circumstance. An exceptionally powerful book!"

Alex Bivens, Ph.D.
Psychologist, Success Coach and Self-Made Millionaire

"While reading this book I found myself weeping as I realized how terribly I have managed money all my life, and that there really is hope. The book provides great awareness and offers simple solutions to a very painful problem—our relationship with money. I loved the principles of financial growth and recovery and found the personal stories powerful, moving and inspiring."

Jaim Hay
President and CEO
OPSA Opinion Publica La Ceiba S.A.

"In the tradition of *Leadership Principles of Attila the Hun* comes *The Financial Wisdom of Ebenezer Scrooge*. By using the beloved Dickens story, the authors provide a wonderful opportunity for readers to transform their relationship with money, and perhaps write a happy ending to their own 'Christmas Carol.'"

Olivia Mellan
Money Psychology Speaker and Author of *Money Harmony,*
Overcoming Overspending and *Money Shy to Money Sure*

"This book is clear, direct and aimed at assisting readers in making progress towards a mindful awareness of their financial energy and deeper enjoyment of life."

Reid Finlayson, M.D.
Assistant Professor of Addiction Medicine and Psychiatry
Vanderbilt University School of Medicine

"These three authors have created a powerful but gentle force for dissolving negative money beliefs and behaviors, and exercises that lead to transformations as big as Ebenezer's."

Susan Bradley
Founder of the Sudden Money Institute & Women, Meaning, and Money

"The importance of understanding the psychology of money is vital to our financial and personal well-being, and yet is so poorly understood by most people. This book provides a very creative, inspirational and practical step-by-step approach to identify what you think about money (money scripts), the maladaptive emotions and behavior associated with irrational thinking about money, and, most important, what you can do to transform your irrational money scripts to financial wisdom."

Steven Miyake, Ph.D.
Clinical Psychologist

"The authors artfully combine their areas of expertise and personal stories with the allegorical lessons of a literary classic. The result is a life-changing guide for all who want to take control of their own financial destinies. I wholeheartedly recommend this book."

Carol Anderson
President
The Money Quotient

"In the first chapter I discovered my money scripts. As I read on I not only was gifted with the hope that my destructive financial self-talk and behaviors could change, but noticed that things actually began changing almost immediately."

Nancy Forhell
A.A. Community College
Severna Park, M.D.

"This is the greatest book I've ever read about money and our relationship to it."

Mauricio Sanhueza, CEO
Sanhueza Psychological Services, Santiago, Chile

"*The Financial Wisdom of Ebenezer Scrooge* is deceptive in its simplistic theme, but will lead you along the complex path the authors refer to as your relationship with money. If you have never thought of money as among your relationships, the perspective offered in this book—through a combination of psychological principles, financial wisdom, literary insights, and personal anecdotes—will surely change your thinking. You may even achieve the transformation the authors seek to facilitate! This book is enriching in ways that money cannot be. It's not too late to add it to your book list for this year, nor to give to a family member about whom you care deeply."

Kathleen M. McNamara, Ph.D.
Clinical Psychologist

"This is a thoughtful, user-friendly and delightful book. It contributes deeply to our understanding of the role(s) of money in our life and brilliantly uses Dickens's *Christmas Carol* story as a guide to a more thriving and abundant life. This will be on my clients' 'must-read' list.

Elizabeth Jetton CFP®
President Financial Vision Advisors, Inc.
Chairperson of The Financial Planning Association

"Finally a book for normal people—over-spenders and hoarders—and everyone in between that hits the nail on the head. This is not your typical money book. What you learn about yourself will surprise you."

Suzi Marsh
LCSW and Host of "Choosing Life: Addictions,
Mental Health & Recovery," 98.5 FM, Atlanta, Georgia

TED KLONTZ, PH.D., RICK KAHLER, CFP®
AND BRAD KLONTZ, PSY.D.

THE
*F*INANCIAL
*W*ISDOM
OF
*E*BENEZER
*S*CROOGE

5 Principles

to Transform Your Relationship

with Money

THE APPROACH FEATURED IN THE WALL STREET JOURNAL

Health Communications, Inc.
Deerfield Beach, Florida

www.bcibooks.com

Library of Congress Cataloging-in-Publication Data

Klontz, Ted.

The financial wisdom of Ebenezer Scrooge : transforming your
   relationship with money / Ted Klontz, Rich Kahler, and Brad Klontz.
      p. cm.
   ISBN-13: 978-0-7573-0354-8
   ISBN-10: 0-7573-0354-4
   1. Finance. Personal—Psychological aspects. 2. Money—Psychological
aspects. 3. Finance, Personal—Decision making. 4. Self-destructive
behavior—Case studies. 5. Self-actualization (Psychology)—Case
studies. I. Title: Transforming your relationship with money.
II. Kahler, Rick. III. Klontz, Brad. IV. Title.
HG179.K574 2005
332.024'001'9—dc22

2005052742

Publisher: Health Communications, Inc.
            3201 S.W. 15th Street
            Deerfield Beach, FL 33442-8190

Cover design by Larissa Hise Henoch
Inside book design by Lawna Patterson Oldfield

CONTENTS

Foreword by Naomi Judd viii

Preface x

Acknowledgments xiii

Introduction: Setting the Stage:
It's Not About the Money xv

1 MONEY SCRIPTS: THE BELIEFS BEHIND THE BEHAVIORS 1

2 MARLEY'S GHOST—STAGE ONE:
DENIAL AND INTERVENTION 33

3 THE FIRST OF THE THREE SPIRITS—STAGE TWO:
EXPLORING THE PAST 53

4 THE SECOND OF THE THREE SPIRITS—STAGE THREE:
UNDERSTANDING THE PRESENT 75

5 THE LAST OF THE THREE SPIRITS—STAGE FOUR:
CONTEMPLATING THE FUTURE 103

6 A NEW SCRIPT—STAGE FIVE: TRANSFORMATION AND
ACTION 111

FOREWORD BY NAOMI JUDD

When you admire someone's wisdom you want to learn all you can from them. Even if it's learning about a topic that typically bores me to sleep, like MONEY. As an avid reader, my preference is non-fiction, particularly psychology and medical. I never considered the topic of money a good read, but when I learned that my life-coach, whom I respect beyond description, had written a book on money I was very curious. As I began to read this book I became totally taken by the message and the methods the authors had used to talk about a subject, the management of which, is a problem for so many of us.

I found myself challenged from time to time with my own thoughts, beliefs and behaviors around money. I got a better understanding of the puzzling money behaviors of those around me. I smiled at some of the real stories that are part of this book and cried at some of the others. I was touched by the authors' honest stories of their own struggles in their relationship with money. I even found myself doing the exercises, thinking about the questions they raise, totally absorbed in the process.

Typical books about money talk about the problem and tell the readers what they should do; basically spend less, save more. Some books go on to provide specific information on which mutual funds, savings accounts and real-estate properties are good investments. Their basic assumption tells the readers that they need to do something and what they do is not enough.

This book is for the multitudes of people who have plenty of information that tells them what they should do but they can't seem to act on the information. For some of us, information is not enough, and more information doesn't help. That's where this book is different because it will show you how to act by unraveling and changing for the better your hidden beliefs about money. Readers will find a number of proven exercises designed to help them move ahead in their quest for financial freedom.

Using their unique experiences, training, backgrounds and clever use of the story of Ebenezer Scrooge's transformation, the authors show readers how to begin to unravel their hidden beliefs called, "money scripts," that are the primary culprits that keep so many people from acting in their own best interest. Best of all, the authors provide the reader practical information about a process of change that can allow them to begin to transform, like Scrooge, their very own lives.

PREFACE

This book is another exciting step in a process and dream that began many years ago.

Though we were unaware of each other's experiences at the time, the three of us had suffered a number of painful events around money, and each of us had decided to find out what part in these events were our responsibility. Independently, we came up with the same general conclusion: "There is something very wrong with my thinking about how all this works." Each of us set out to find out what was wrong.

A couple of years later, the three of us, all having had similar thoughts and awarenesses, met in the Black Hills of South Dakota and began talking about putting together a process that would combine our experiences, thoughts, dreams and gifts. The result was a unique workshop designed to blend the fields of financial planning and psychology. Our first workshop, held in September 2003, was featured by Jeff Zaslow in his *Wall Street Journal* column, "Moving On."

The experiences and life-changing results for the participants in that initial workshop were more profound than we could have imagined. One of the first comments from the participants was "Where's the book?" At Brad's prompting, we decided to begin writing a book about our concept. Since Brad is a published researcher, we also decided to begin a research study, one of the very few related to changing clients' money beliefs and behaviors. We wanted to determine whether what we were doing in our work with people could stand up to the rigors of scientific investigation. We are currently completing the final phase of that study, which has yielded some groundbreaking results.

We spent the next several months full of excitement, yet struggling to find a way to give form to a relatively simple sounding, yet surprisingly complex, concept: blending from psychology what we know about how people think, make decisions and change, with the relatively straightforward process of financial planning.

The idea of *A Christmas Carol* being a vehicle to deliver our concepts appeared when we least expected it, in a place not normally thought to be one of the great sites for idea creation. We were sitting in the rocking chairs at Nashville's metropolitan airport talking about a totally different topic when Ted said, "It's the *Christmas Carol*! That is the perfect vehicle to use to help us explain what we do and what we see happening with the clients we work with!"

After more than one strange look, and more than a few

moments of explanation, we all got the vision and went back to study *A Christmas Carol* to find out just how much we could integrate what we do with Dickens's classic tale. Surprised at the number of parallels we saw, we began pouring our energy into creating what you will read in this book.

We all went our separate ways to develop our thoughts, then put them together one day a couple of months later on Grady Cash's basement wall. There he began to block out the random thoughts from three would-be authors into a form that we all then took and worked from.

Finally, Carolyn Linn thankfully agreed to sign on as our developmental editor and further helped us make sure that what we were thinking matched what we were writing. Working with one of us is bad enough. As they say, there will be a special place in heaven for people like her.

We sincerely hope that when you read this book, the transformations we have seen take place in ourselves and others will also happen for you.

ACKNOWLEDGMENTS

We would like to thank those who so willingly gave their time and opinions as we floated around various concepts, ideas and our early editions of the manuscript. Wonderful responses from dozens of clients were invaluable, and though for confidentiality reasons we can't name them publicly, we can thank them publicly. You know who you are. Thank you!

Thank you, also, to the clients who allowed us to use their personal stories as illustrations. All the examples and stories we have used in this book are true, but, except for our own, the names have been changed.

Peter Vegso, Gary Seidler and Allison Janse of HCI (Health Communications, Inc.) were very instrumental in the creation of this book by being willing to trust three unknown writers who had this wild idea about financial wisdom and Ebenezer Scrooge.

Versions of two of the stories in this book, "Angels

Dancing" and "Twenty-Four Hours to Live," have been published previously in *Chicken Soup for the Recovering Soul* (HCI, 2005) and appear here with permission.

In researching for this book, we found Michael Patrick Hearn's *The Annotated Christmas Carol* (W. W. Norton & Company, 2004) most helpful in providing background information on the life and times of Charles Dickens. We highly recommend it to those readers who would like to learn more.

We met in wonderful places—Nashville, the Black Hills of South Dakota and Kauai, Hawaii (our personal favorite)—to work on this book. We want to thank our very tolerant partners and soul mates—Margie, Marcia and Joni—and other family members—including Brenda, Wanda, Jim and Diane—who honored, supported and encouraged us with their patience as well as insightful and important feedback during the various edits as this book was being written. They were willing to sacrifice precious family and vacation time and energy, while providing food and emotional support, hosting us and otherwise helping us with this project.

INTRODUCTION

SETTING THE STAGE:
IT'S NOT ABOUT THE MONEY

*It is impossible to achieve ultimate
meaning from that which
cannot give ultimate meaning.*

—JACOB NEEDLEMAN
Money and the Meaning of Life

❧⚜❧

"Merry Christmas, uncle."
"Bah! Humbug! What right do you have to be
merry? You're poor enough."
"What right do you have to be so dismal?
You're rich enough."
"Bah!" said Scrooge again. "Humbug!"

—*A Christmas Carol*

Scrooge was a miser, to begin with. There is no doubt whatever about that.

No one with even a vague familiarity with Charles Dickens's classic *A Christmas Carol,* the story of penny-pinching Ebenezer Scrooge, could argue with such a statement about the tale's main character.

Scrooge was a miserable man who seemingly had enough money to be more than comfortable. Still, he dipped his own candles, kept his sparse apartment cold and dark, cared nothing about the welfare of others and worried endlessly that someone would take advantage of him and his wealth.

Dickens describes him as a man whose heart was so cold he was even unaffected by the weather:

> *"No warmth could warm, nor wintry weather chill him.*
> *No wind that blew was bitterer than he."*

Yet, before the tale is over, Scrooge experiences profound changes in his outlook and behavior. By the final chapter, he is transformed into a joyful, compassionate, generous man.

What happened? Scrooge became a new man because he took a difficult journey. It wasn't a journey he took willingly, but as the night wore on, he became more eager to learn the life-changing lessons the spirits had to teach.

Scrooge's enlightenment begins with an intervention, a visit from the ghost of his old business partner, Jacob Marley. It continues with the wise guidance of the Ghost of Christmas Past. Scrooge sees how past events from his childhood created beliefs about money and attitudes that were destroying his life and keeping him spiritually and emotionally poor in spite of his great wealth. Next, the Ghost of Christmas Present models the true abundance that is so lacking in Scrooge's life and shows Scrooge the reality of the world and how he fits into it. Finally, the Ghost of Christmas Future shows Scrooge what the consequences will be if he doesn't change.

By visiting his past, clearly seeing the present and understanding the consequences of the future, Scrooge brings his life into balance. Most of all, he becomes happy, at peace with himself and with the world.

The root of Scrooge's miserly existence was an unhealthy belief system about money. In spite of his wealth, Scrooge's beliefs about money—created, nurtured and anchored in his long-forgotten past—kept him poor in spirit. His loyal employee, Bob Cratchit, also had some unhealthy beliefs about money that contributed to his poverty. Like Scrooge and Cratchit, who represent two extremes, many people are trapped by money beliefs they are unaware of. They irrationally continue destructive behaviors, unable to break free and recognize how they are sabotaging their own goals and dreams.

This classic tale of how one man finds his true course in life provides a powerful model that we can still learn from today. Not only was Dickens a master storyteller, he had insights into human behavior—and how to change it—that were far ahead of his time. To help Scrooge on his journey from misery to enlightenment, the spirits skillfully use techniques that are employed by modern psychologists and financial planners.

As the story of *A Christmas Carol* unfolds, Scrooge learns five principles that lead to financial wisdom. In this book we share this wisdom. We have seen it transform careers, families and lives. Don't think that these principles work only for the wealthy. You will soon come to understand that the amount of money you have or make is irrelevant. It's not about the money. It's the relationship you have with money that is the key.

By applying these principles to your life, you can move from denial to awareness, from destructive behaviors to productive behaviors, from misery to joy. You can become a new person.

Scrooge changed . . . and so can you!

One of the most profound truths in this book is that as long as there is life, it is possible to change. It is never too late. The peace and joy that Scrooge finds is possible for all of us.

The answers that you—and millions like you—are seeking can be found in *The Financial Wisdom of Ebenezer Scrooge.*

Self-Defeating Behaviors

Most people remember Ebenezer Scrooge as stingy, cold, abusive, uncaring, cruel, lonely and obsessed with money. Of course, no one would voluntarily choose to be such a pitiable person, and Scrooge didn't consciously choose to be a miserable old miser. Like many people today, Scrooge lived his life in a significant amount of pain caused by numerous hidden beliefs about money that were not serving him well.

Yet in all fairness, Scrooge has positive qualities. He is thrifty, certainly, and good in business. He is also intelligent, disciplined, skilled, honest and persistent. Even so, when we first meet Scrooge, he is a miserable human being.

Scrooge's hidden beliefs about money are at the root of his misery.

Scrooge is not the only character in *A Christmas Carol*

whose hidden beliefs about money do not serve him well. Bob Cratchit, Scrooge's clerk and father of Tiny Tim, lived in as much misery as his employer. While Cratchit, too, has positive attributes, such as being loyal, caring, forgiving, kind, spiritual and a good father, he also suffers from self-destructive beliefs about money. He lacks the ability to imagine what he might do differently to change his plight. Scrooge underpays him, yet he makes no effort to seek better employment. He overspends for Christmas dinner, splurging over a week's pay on the goose.

Even allowing for a socioeconomic environment that would have made a change of employment very difficult, it seems fair to say that his self-defeating beliefs and behaviors around money kept him a prisoner of his plight, serving a life sentence of misery.

Scrooge and Cratchit Behaviors Exist Today

There are millions of modern-day examples of people who, like Scrooge and Cratchit, are imprisoned by self-defeating money behaviors. We don't have to look very far or hard to see them. Few have the skills to actually alter their basic money behaviors, even when they know that their money habits are limiting or even harming their lives. Signs of this suffering are everywhere.

***CAROL* TRIVIA**

Tiny Tim runs to Scrooge and they walk away hand in hand in the final scene of *Scrooge,* the 1951 black-and-white film classic. Since Tiny Tim does recover with support from Scrooge, his illness was obviously treatable. From his symptoms, pediatric physicians surmise that Tiny Tim had a kidney disease that made his blood too acidic. Recovery would have been rapid with a better diet and alkaline solutions commonly used by physicians in 1843.

The Scrooges of our modern-day world, in spite of their wealth, also find ways to unconsciously sabotage their lives. We see them often in our work:

- Workaholics who become estranged from their families or divorce because of their beliefs about what enough money is and/or what money can and cannot provide.
- People who continue, year after year, to work at jobs they hate, with the hope that the money they earn or accumulate will eventually bring them fulfillment or meaning.
- Recipients of financial windfalls who discover that wealth brings new problems, rather than the peace and comfort they anticipated.
- Those who are so afraid of losing money that they can't stop for a single moment to enjoy life.
- Wealthy individuals who are guilt ridden about their money.

The Cratchits of the world, broadly defined as those who choose to be underachievers, cannot live within their means and/or are failing to prepare for their future. We recognize them because they are

- Drowning in credit card debt, which is currently at record highs.
- Experiencing the shame of bankruptcy, which exceeds 1.5 million new filings each year—one every fifteen seconds.
- Finding it impossible to save money.
- Facing retirement with insufficient funds.
- Spending their discretionary income on luxuries rather than necessities.
- Threatening their primary relationships with constant disagreements over money.
- Allowing their fear of financial loss to keep them from making investments. Instead, they put their money in savings accounts, low-interest CDs or even shoeboxes around the house. Consequently, inflation and taxation will doom them to the very future they're striving so fearfully to avoid.

In March 2004, a survey commissioned by the American Psychological Association showed that 72 percent of Americans report that money is their number-one stressor, ahead of issues such as work, physical health and children.

The list goes on.

Millions of people are self-destructive when it comes to money. Like Scrooge and Cratchit, they think the problem *is* money.

It's not.

Don't misunderstand and think money isn't important. It is! However, a wealthy client of ours once told us, "I don't know if it is more of a curse to have too little money or too much."

> **It is hard to tell what does bring happiness;**
> **poverty and wealth have both failed.**
>
> —*Kin Hubbard (1868–1930)*

The truth is, people from all socioeconomic levels are trapped in self-destructive behaviors that feel right to them. Whether or not they know they need to change, they have been unable to do so.

We have been able to help many of them through our financial therapy, coaching and workshops. The key is opening their eyes to the fact that money is not the issue. At the core of their behaviors is an unhealthy belief system about money that they are often unaware of because this system doesn't *feel* unhealthy; it feels right. These beliefs—created, nurtured and anchored in their childhoods—are driving their behaviors and keeping them poor.

Your beliefs—even those you aren't aware of—drive your behaviors, too. If you know something with your head and still can't make lasting changes in your behavior, it's because your hidden beliefs are really in control of your behavior. Acting contrary to these hidden beliefs is uncomfortable.

Understanding this truth and being willing to uncover those hidden beliefs is fundamental to the process of freeing yourself from unwanted behaviors.

Beliefs drive behaviors.

Your behaviors are driven by your true beliefs. The advice, "Do what I say, not what I do," acknowledges the truth that we often don't follow what we know is the best course of action. The goal of this book is to help you identify those hidden beliefs that are sabotaging your fulfillment in life, bring them into full awareness and deal with them—so that they will lose their power. If you do this successfully, you will be able to regain control of your life and consciously *choose* the beliefs you will live by.

Chapter 1 examines some of the more common of these beliefs, which we call "money scripts," and contains exercises to help you identify yours. We—the three authors—have all struggled with our own limiting beliefs, and we will share our stories and those of our clients to help you along the path to financial enlightenment. Many of you, for example, will relate to Brad's story.

Not Me . . . I Am Going to Do It Differently
by BRADLEY T. KLONTZ, PSY.D.

As a clinical psychologist, I am an expert in human behavior. In addition to many years of rigorous academic and clinical study, I have spent much time and effort recovering from my own emotional wounds. I have a very good understanding of how thoughts, feelings, family histories and unfinished business affect a person's functioning, and I have been able to help many people change. That is part of what makes the rest of this story a bit ironic.

I was born into a poor family. We have been poor for generations. My father, who you will learn more about later in this book when you read his story, grew up on a small farm in Ohio. As the story goes, the farm was single-handedly saved by his grandfather's hard work during the Great Depression. My dad was the oldest of three children. Once a week he bathed in an outdoor tub heated with water from the coal stove, and he had the honor of being the second person in line to use the bathwater. Some argue his younger brother, my uncle, as the third child, often came out of the tub dirtier than when he went in.

Cornmeal mush was a delicacy, and sometimes lunch consisted of sugar between two pieces of bread. Each child received two pairs of blue jeans each fall to last the year.

My father was just the second of his extended family to receive a college education. Although he secured a job as a teacher, he still considered himself poor. During my childhood, we spent many years living in other people's houses. Eventually, he was able to purchase a house, but since it was a fixer-upper and he had no money, it didn't have any interior walls for several years, only studs where the walls would be some day.

While I was oblivious to it as a child, I learned later in life that my father suffered from what he now calls "poor thinking." He didn't see that he had other options; nor did he believe he deserved anything better. While the thought of creating a better life may have crossed his mind, he didn't know what to do about it. He thought, "If only the school system would pay me more," believing, like many of his peers, that someone or something external to himself held the key to a better life. Even so, he struggled with guilt because he was living much better than most of his extended family members.

As a result of his poor thinking, my father consistently worked for much less than he was worth, did not save and did not take even moderate risks with what little money he accidentally accumulated. After all, we were poor people, from generations of poor people. He could not imagine any other way of living. As I was growing up, I decided *Not me! I am going to do it differently!*

My mother's family migrated to Detroit in the 1940s in pursuit of work. They were part of the Appalachian migration to urban industrial centers. The youngest of three girls, my mother grew up in a working class neighborhood bordering the projects in Detroit, Michigan.

My grandfather worked at a General Motors plant. In the interest of home defense, he purchased a series of firearms over the years to protect his family from the frequent break-ins in the community. Despite his efforts, criminals repeatedly stole from his home, including, among other things, his latest firearm purchases. My grandfather died in his nineties with a loaded rifle within reach of his bed.

After losing what little money they had in banks during the Great Depression, my grandfather kept his money in a strongbox in the attic. My mother grew up with a mistrust of financial institutions also. Why wouldn't she? She went to a school that combined children from a poor neighborhood and children from a wealthier neighborhood. She was very aware early on that she was in a lower socioeconomic class, and she felt inferior as a result. As an adult, my mother was a saver but put her money in very low risk investments, and as a part-time teacher, she gave me the message throughout my childhood that we indeed were poor. But as I was growing up, I decided *Not me! I am going to do it differently!*

Although my family would have qualified as lower-middle class, I grew up believing we were poor. In retrospect, we were poor, in the worst way: in our thinking. I felt shame about my limited opportunities and limited experiences. Many of my classmates and colleagues came from more economically advantaged backgrounds, only furthering my sense of alienation and shame. So I vowed, with much determination, to do it differently.

And I did do it differently. And it cost me dearly.

When I finally graduated from a decade of postsecondary education, I became an investor. Without any training or functional knowledge about finances or the stock market, I began buying and selling stocks. For me, the real risk was that I felt I was not taking any risks. However, in the two years following the tech bubble implosion in 2000, I lost over half the money I initially invested. This was a life-changing experience for me. I felt a great deal of pain and shame.

I had no conscious understanding about my hidden generational beliefs and my personal relationship with money. In trying to "do it differently" than my parents, I made a big mistake and ended up just like them, with little money. Fortunately, my experiences in my own emotional recovery had taught me to look for assistance and more information when I find myself in pain. Experiencing this pain opened my eyes. So began my journey of financial recovery.

My pain woke me up to the fact that I needed more accurate information and help. When the opportunity arose for me to attend a workshop, facilitated by coauthor Rick Kahler, exploring my own relationship with money, I leapt at it. Interestingly, my father, step-mother and fiancée were also in attendance. At one point, we were asked to talk about the messages we received about money from our families. My father volunteered to speak about the messages he received, and as he spoke, I sat in my chair with my jaw hanging open, while my fiancée gently poked me in the ribs with each point he made. While he had never spoken these words to me, the message had trickled down, and almost every thought he shared was something she had heard me say about money!

Getting a grasp on the profound influence these entrenched generational money messages had on my daily behavior and self-talk around money was a life-changing experience for me. As I began to work with the feelings connected to my experiences and thoughts, feelings such as hurt, guilt and shame, I grew increasingly able to separate myself from my thoughts. Gradually, this distance allowed me to think more objectively. Now when these old money scripts arise, I no longer respond automatically and unconsciously. I am able to challenge the validity of my thinking as it is occurring. As a result, I am able to make more balanced decisions. When I find myself in an unusually difficult or stressful financial situation, or when I am struggling with some outdated or painful money scripts, I enlist the help and guidance of others. By so doing, I am able to make much more balanced and healthy decisions around money.

For example, periodically I begin to think that I am not working hard enough or making enough money. In my family, being thought of as lazy is probably the worst insult one can receive. I have been able to identify this as a generational money script, and I am aware that it was around long before I was, so it isn't about me. I am also aware that living with this message as if it were true has bred generations of workaholics that sacrifice self, relationships and pleasure in the never-ending pursuit of working "hard enough." Nevertheless, despite this knowledge, this thought periodically sneaks into my consciousness. In the past, I would take it to heart, resulting in feelings of guilt, shame and self-loathing. In an attempt to feel better, I would work harder and longer hours. If I didn't, I'd pay the price of feeling like a lazy, no-good failure. In my best moments, I am now able to separate myself from this thought and therefore not respond automatically by overworking. In my worst moments, I have difficulty letting it go.

When that happens, I seek a reality check from someone close to me. Typically, an objective review of how much I am actually working and a reminder of what I value most and refuse to compromise for the sake of more money (i.e., my relationships to self and others) quickly reorganizes my thoughts. When this shift occurs, the feelings of guilt and shame subside, and I am able to make behavioral choices consistent with my true values and goals.

Now, I *am* doing it differently.

Scrooge's Example

The story of Ebenezer Scrooge's journey to a life free of his destructive beliefs and behaviors around money is a powerful model for us today. The journey he takes follows the same steps, or stages, that we teach.

Rather than chapters, Dickens called the divisions of his book *staves*, a term for the five horizontal lines on which musical notes are written, since the tale is, after all, a Christmas carol. Each stave illustrates a necessary stage on the path to Scrooge's enlightenment:

Stave 1. Marley's Ghost	Stage 1. Denial and Intervention
Stave 2. The First of the Three Spirits	Stage 2. Exploring the Past
Stave 3. The Second of the Three Spirits	Stage 3. Understanding the Present
Stave 4. The Last of the Spirits	Stage 4. Contemplating the Future
Stave 5. The End of It	Stage 5. Transformation and Action

We call our "staves" the "five stages." These stages are the core of the Klontz-Kahler model of financial integration, enlightenment and peace that has brought transformation to so many of our clients and workshop participants—just as they enabled Scrooge to transform from a miserable miser to a joyful man of compassion. There are important lessons for all of us at each stage, lessons we call the "Principles of Financial Wisdom." These five principles will guide you on your own journey.

Applying the Wisdom of the Introduction

1. Both Scrooge and Cratchit lived miserable lives, and their un-conscious beliefs about money were at the root of their misery. What aspects of your life are you less than satisfied with? How might your beliefs about money be affecting them?

2. Think about an issue in your life in which spending, lack of saving, keeping secrets about money or some other money behavior is making you feel uncomfortable. Imagine for a moment that these uncomfortable feelings aren't about the money. What really might be at their core?

3. What are all the phrases that come to mind when you complete this sentence: "Money is . . . ?" Write down as many things that come to mind as quickly as possible.

1

MONEY SCRIPTS

THE BELIEFS BEHIND THE BEHAVIORS

If you bring forth what is within you, what you have will save you.

—THE GNOSTIC GOSPEL OF ST. THOMAS

As warped as Scrooge's behavior may seem, his actions make perfect sense when viewed in the context of his beliefs about money. Several hidden beliefs are at the root of Scrooge's misery. For example, Scrooge believed "You can't trust anyone with your money." He didn't even trust his loyal clerk, Bob Cratchit. We can see this clearly in the first chapter of *A Christmas Carol*:

> *"The door of Scrooge's counting house was open*
> *that he might keep his eye upon his clerk."*

Scrooge also believed that you "Don't spend money on yourself or others." He lived this belief to the extreme. He barely heated his office and lit his sparse apartment with a single candle:

> *"Darkness is cheap, and Scrooge liked it."*

These and other similar behaviors certainly appear severe, but not when you look at his perspective of the world. In view of these underlying and mostly unconscious beliefs, Scrooge's actions are perfectly logical, at least from his perspective. In our work, we have come to believe that every financial behavior, no matter how seemingly illogical, makes perfect sense when we understand the underlying beliefs. Scrooge's excessive behaviors merely reflected what he believed to be true.

We call these powerful beliefs *money scripts.*

Money Scripts

Very early in life, people begin to internalize messages about money's purpose—how it works, what it promises, its overall significance—and develop their relationship to it. Since children can't fully grasp adult reality, they translate what they see and hear into unconscious rules about life, including any internalized messages about money. These messages about money, or money scripts, don't necessarily reflect reality from the adult perspective. Instead, they may represent only a distorted or partial truth as seen through the eyes of a child. As children grow into adulthood, they often behave as though these partial truths are absolute truths. They may find themselves unable to change destructive behaviors that, at a very basic level, somehow feel right and make perfect sense.

Think of a money script like the script for a play with several roles in it. The script is written by one person, and a specific role in the script is memorized by another person—an actor who plays one character in that particular play. If the actor memorizes the script and executes his lines well, the result will be exactly what the playwright intended. However, if the actor attempts to use the same script for any other role, or in any other play, the results will be disastrous. It is the same with money scripts.

To learn their lines, actors must repeat them over and over. Few actors, no matter how talented, can read a script once and then deliver a flawless performance. They must practice frequently. In a similar way, the depth of any money script depends on the frequency and intensity of the original event or financial trauma. A child who hears his mother voice concern once about how the family business may fail and that they may not have money for food will probably not internalize a damaging money script. However, if the child hears his mother voice that fear monthly, weekly or daily, the result could be a deeply held belief that will influence the child's behavior well into adulthood. Our deepest, most ingrained money scripts are often formed by such examples of financial trauma.

For example, when Brenda was eight years old, she, unlike the rest of her siblings, saved her money. When the rest of the family needed money, they robbed her piggy bank.

Sounds sad but innocent enough, right? But little Brenda internalized the same message that Scrooge internalized: "You can't trust anyone with your money." This worked for both Scrooge and Brenda as children. However, as adults, the results of this money script didn't work for either of them—although the results for Brenda were very different from Scrooge's.

As an adult, Brenda earns $250,000 a year. She needs only $100,000 to support her preferred lifestyle, but she spends the entire amount each year. She doesn't use many of the things she buys. She spends all of her money rather than saves or invests it because of an unconscious fear that others will take it away. This old belief is reinforced when her parents and siblings frequently call and want her to bail them out of some financial dilemma. By never having any money in the bank, she can say no when her siblings ask her for money. Unfortunately, spending money as quickly as she gets it makes her just like them—always broke.

**Money scripts internalized in childhood
can affect our beliefs and behaviors
well into adulthood.**

Why Money Scripts Are So Powerful

Brenda's belief, originating from a child's perspective of an experience, created a money script that is still affecting her today. Brenda's subconscious belief is keeping her from achieving success. She neglects to save for her future. So, while she is enjoying the fruits of her labors, her inability to say no to her family and her failure to save jeopardize her financial future. Worse, because it is mostly unconscious, Brenda isn't even aware that this money script is sabotaging her career goals and dreams for her own family. Instead, she feels a vague sense of dissatisfaction and failure because she knows she should be saving and investing for her future, but can't.

When we met Brenda, she thought the answer to saving money was to earn more; *then* she could save. The problem was that she had been saying the same thing to herself as she moved up the salary scale from $50,000 to $100,000 to $150,000 to $250,000. To us, it was obvious that the solution lay elsewhere, in her basic money script.

> **People are generally unaware of their money scripts and how their self-defeating behaviors are linked to them.**

Often, these messages learned during childhood are buried so deeply that the individual doesn't know about or question the belief, even when acting on it causes him or her repeated problems.

It is important to understand that money scripts are not inherently good or bad, right or wrong. Certain money scripts can serve us well when applied to the appropriate financial circumstance. However, money scripts can become a problem, even become destructive, when they are applied to inappropriate financial circumstances.

For example, have you ever met anyone with this money script:

> *"I deserve to spend money on myself."*

Now, believing you deserve to spend money on yourself is

not inherently bad. In fact, it can be very positive. We hope you believe this to be true. Many people do not share this belief, but we all deserve to take care of ourselves. Nevertheless, believing you deserve something extravagant for yourself today at the expense of saving for tomorrow can undermine your financial well-being.

Moreover, believing that you deserve to spend money on yourself to the point that you feel entitled to do so regardless of your circumstances can also be destructive. Professional credit counselors tell us that this is a typical money script among people with excessive debt. Some of their stories of money mismanagement are incredible.

Carl had serious credit problems. Quite unexpectedly, he received a windfall inheritance. He could have used it to pay off his debt. He could have saved it. He could have used it to rebuild his life. Instead, he bought a new car. He threw a big party, bought new clothes and gave money away. Within months, he was back in the same predicament. This is not an isolated example. Dave Ramsey, a nationally syndicated radio talk-show host, author and founder of Financial Peace University, has cited statistics showing that within seven years of coming into money, the average person, like Carl, will be living at the same economic level as they were before the windfall appeared.

This behavior seems incredibly destructive, yet it makes sense to the person whose money script is "I deserve to spend money on myself." Having that money script creates the same consequences that would have occurred if the person had made a conscious decision to be poor.

Money Scripts Are Generational

Frequently, our money scripts are passed down through the generations. When people carefully explore their family histories, clear and profound patterns of financial behaviors often emerge. With close examination of our multigenerational family stories, we are able to identify the money scripts driving the actions of our ancestors. Many of us live our financial lives unaware of how powerfully our beliefs around money are linked to the specific experiences of our ancestors. As such, they continue to affect us today, long after their adaptive and functional aspects have lost their benefit.

In our work with clients, we still see in today's forty- to sixty-year-olds the lessons their parents and grandparents learned during the Great Depression. Hiding money, hoarding money, not trusting banks or investment institutions, and poverty thinking are behaviors that still plague the children and grandchildren of family members traumatized by those economic and social experiences.

Younger clients suffer from other thinking distortions. One father told us of his uneasiness as he handed his eight-year-old daughter her twenty-dollar-a-week allowance. He sensed that the amount was too much, but he didn't want her to feel different from the other kids in the neighborhood whose parents gave their eight-year-olds that amount.

Another parent told of his distress in realizing that his seven-year-old had no idea where money comes from or what is involved in acquiring it. He learned this when he told her she could not have something she wanted because there was no money for it. Her response was, "Daddy, just go to the wall and get some." She had learned that money comes from "the wall," better known to adults as an ATM. In fact, we have worked with a number of clients who tell us that one of their beliefs is that "Money is not real." Since it is not real, then there is nothing to deal with.

Money scripts and their consequences, such as the ones we have mentioned, are much more of a potential problem than ever. Two generations ago, if you got a good job, worked hard and were a loyal employee, at the end of twenty-five, thirty or forty years of service, you received an adequate guaranteed retirement. That, along with Social Security, would pretty much guarantee you would have sufficient funds for the rest of your life. Now, however, both corporate America and the Social Security system have changed radically. Fewer companies offer defined benefits retirement plans. Fewer employees choose or even have the option of lifetime employment. And the Social Security system is bending and threatening to collapse under the weight of too many recipients, too few contributors and the extended life spans of the beneficiaries. Given this reality, old money scripts and their resulting behaviors can be disastrous.

Knowledge Is Power

The following sections examine the money scripts driving Scrooge, Cratchit and many people today. Armed with this knowledge, you'll be ready to begin recognizing at least some of your own money scripts. In some cases, awareness, along with a commitment to change, is enough to change behavior that is being driven by an unconscious belief and can help clear the way for conscious beliefs to move into the driver's seat.

Scrooge Chose to Be Poor

As we've mentioned, despite his great wealth, Ebenezer Scrooge unconsciously chose to be poor. Of course, if the definition of poor were measured solely by one's bank account, Scrooge would certainly not fit that definition. On the other hand, if you define poor as a measure of the quality of one's physical environment, emotional health, relationship quality and lifestyle, then Scrooge would certainly qualify as poor. Scrooge's excessive hoarding created an impoverishment as real as any caused by financial distress. Ironically, Scrooge's money scripts created the very poverty and isolation that Young Scrooge had so desperately tried to avoid.

- As an apprentice under Fezziwig, Young Scrooge had to sleep under a counter at the warehouse. As an adult, Scrooge lives in a dreary old apartment that was as cold and sparse as a warehouse.

- As a child, Scrooge spent the holidays alone at the warehouse. As an adult, Scrooge spends the holidays alone in his rooms.
- As a child, Scrooge was poor. As an adult, Scrooge lives a meager existence, eating sparingly and barely heating or lighting his tiny dwelling.

Scrooge lived in a poverty created by his own beliefs and behaviors around money.

Scrooge's Money Scripts

As we observe Scrooge's behaviors, we can begin to see the money scripts that drove them. These are just a few of Scrooge's money scripts:

- You can't trust anyone with your money.
- People only want you for your money.
- You must work hard for money.
- You can never have enough money.
- Don't spend money on yourself or others.
- Money will give you meaning in life.
- The more money you have, the happier you will be.
- You can never be happy if you are poor.
- Giving to the poor encourages laziness.
- If you had more money, things would be better.

Scrooge was living in harmony with what he believed to be true. Unfortunately, many of his beliefs about money were distorted half-truths. As a result, he was living a life full of pain and loneliness and devoid of love.

Your money scripts could be
keeping you financially, emotionally
or spiritually poor.

Similarly, your money scripts could be the reason you are in debt, facing bankruptcy and living in deprivation. Your money scripts could be sabotaging your quest for the American dream, your retirement, your children's education and your financial security. Even if you have significant wealth, your money scripts could be destroying your peace of mind, relationships, happiness and sense of fulfillment.

Cratchit Chose to Be Poor

One could argue that Bob Cratchit, Scrooge's loyal clerk and father of Tiny Tim, was a victim of circumstance. He was trapped in an abusive socioeconomic system that didn't allow the less fortunate individual to advance. On the other hand, we would argue that Cratchit's unconscious money scripts contributed to his poverty. He didn't truly appreciate his own talents and skills. He undersold himself. He spent impulsively when he could have bought medicine for his son. He didn't know what steps to take to plan for his own future.

In effect, it's possible that Cratchit made an unconscious decision to be poor.

Cratchit's Money Scripts

Bob Cratchit is often characterized as the eternal optimist, always finding the silver lining in a bad situation. But careful analysis of his behavior reveals there's far more to his personality.

Bob Cratchit also has his share of money scripts. Although Dickens never tells us the nature of Tiny Tim's illness, we know that it is treatable. Yet Cratchit spends his money on a goose for Christmas dinner instead of buying medicine for Tiny Tim—a classic example of binge spending.

Carol Trivia

In today's dollars, Bob Cratchit's Christmas dinner would have cost about $500. His spending for Christmas dinner was considered so extravagant that in some early stage adaptations, the goose becomes a surprise gift from Scrooge's nephew, Fred.

Cratchit stays in a minimum wage job working for Scrooge when he might have found better employment elsewhere. Rather than even thinking about improving his situation, Cratchit stays stuck and unaware of his choices. Even when his family mocks Scrooge, Cratchit defends and protects him. He accepts his miserable existence as his destiny.

Let's look at a few of Bob Cratchit's possible money scripts:

- There will never be enough money.
- Money is to be spent, not saved.
- You'll be paid what you are worth.
- You can never be happy if you are rich.
- If you are good, the universe will supply your needs.
- You don't deserve money.

It's easy to see how Cratchit's unconscious money scripts, as we have defined them, keep him stuck in the role of a victim, trapped in poverty. His family supports this belief by reinforcing that Scrooge was the problem, not Bob.

It's easier to be a victim than to change one's behavior.

Money Scripts and the Truth

One reason that some money scripts are so difficult to change is that, like the broken clock that's accurate twice a day, a money script that is dysfunctional in one situation can be functional in another. The fact that most scripts are valid part of the time makes it harder for people to recognize that they may be applying the same money scripts inappropriately. In other words, sometimes "true" is not always true.

For example, if you were approached by a con artist promoting a get-rich-quick scheme, a money script of "trust no one" would prevent a disastrous money mistake. The problem arises when you apply that same script to a scrupulous financial planner, attorney, accountant or even your spouse. That's like an actor playing the same role, regardless of whether the movie is a comedy, drama or adventure. The role needs to change to fit the situation. It's the same with money scripts.

Paul, for example, believed that "being in debt is like being in prison." Understanding that debt is a significant obligation is important. Because this script was so entrenched within him, however, Paul was never able to buy a home for his family because he could never save enough to pay cash for it. As a result, he and his family had lived in a series of rented apartments and homes for over twenty years, actually spending more on rent payments than he would have on house payments if he had taken out a loan. Even when loan rates were the lowest they had been in over fifty years, Paul could not take advantage of this favorable financial opportunity because he "didn't want to go to prison."

Of the eighty or more money scripts Kate identified for herself, the one that was "absolutely true" was "the only thing a parent can give a child that can't be taken away is an education at a private school." The tuition to send Kate's children to private elementary and prep schools consumed over 20 percent of her family's income. Still, Kate was driven by this money script, although the public schools in her area were above average, her children said they would prefer to go to public school and her graduating son had received a full scholarship to a state university. Kate and her husband were spending so much on the children's education that there was no money left for them to save for their retirement or even pay the interest on their mortgage. Kate's dream of improving her employment situation by obtaining a much-needed master's degree was completely shelved.

While it appears obvious to you and me that Kate could not afford private schools and that Kate's children would probably not suffer significantly by attending public schools, she was unable to see it any other way.

Same Money Script, Different Manifestations

You'd think that the same money script held by two different people would lead to the same behaviors for each person. Interestingly, as we saw in Brenda's case, it does not. Behaviors can vary widely depending on how a money script manifests itself. For example, consider the money script "If only I had more money, I would be happy."

To obtain money, and thus happiness, some people might

turn into workaholics. Others might become obsessive underspenders or hoarders. Some might turn to unethical or illegal actions. Some might turn to gambling. Others might take excessive risks with their money, chasing get-rich-quick schemes. Others, sensing they will never be able to have enough, may become chronically underemployed and feel hopeless and depressed. Whatever is desired—fulfillment, happiness or security—will always remain just out of reach.

On the other hand—and only up to a point—having more money can open up more opportunities and create more happiness and fulfillment in someone's life. A *TIME* poll conducted by SRBI Public Affairs in December 2004 showed that there is a direct correlation between income and happiness until a person reaches an income of $50,000 annually. Above that threshold, however, there is no significant increase in happiness as earnings rise.

Common Money Scripts

Unconscious money scripts and the behaviors they engender are sabotaging the goals and dreams of many.

Walk through a mall on any weekend. You'll see people buying things they really don't need and they probably can't afford. Others stay in jobs they hate because they convince themselves "It can't get any better than this for me." Consider Charles.

Charles has worked in public education for thirty-five years and complains about the lack of personal challenge and

mistreatment by the system. Though he grumbles constantly, he resists all opportunities to understand his options and alter his fate. This resistance is unconscious on Charles's part. He cannot see how the skills he's developed over his thirty-five-year career are transferable to other careers. He thinks others can make such a transition, but he cannot. When we suggested that such a change would be possible, and that, in fact, one of us had done so coming out of the same profession, his response was "Maybe you can, but not me."

Nor is wealth an inoculation against destructive money scripts. We consistently see wealthy people who are trapped by their money scripts. One common mistake they make is trying to buy fulfillment, whether by buying the newest luxury car or fashion, or by giving too much to friends, relatives or children. Another of the wealthy's self-destructive money scripts involves guilt over having wealth when others don't. One of our client couples told us that they feel shame when they are around peers who are wealthier, because they haven't done well enough, and they feel guilt around people who have less than they do. The only people that they feel comfortable with are those who have about the same amount as they do, giving them a relatively small and limited number of choices.

People acting on their unconscious money scripts are ubiquitous. Look at how your parents, your friends and even your own children behave around money. You'll see obvious mistakes. Why do people continue behaviors that are so harmful to themselves and their loved ones? Why can't they

see their mistakes? Why do they behave so irrationally? What drives these obviously destructive behaviors? Why are these money scripts so powerful? To find out, let's analyze some common money scripts.

1. "Money is bad."

Many variations of this script exist:

• "The rich are greedy/shallow/insensitive."
• "If you have money, you got it by taking advantage of others."
• "Money is evil."

The message here is that having money is bad, unspiritual or even evil. The assumption is that rich people did something bad to obtain wealth. Therefore, if you obtain wealth, you are a bad person.

> **Rich people are "bad." Therefore, if I
> became wealthy, I will be bad, too.**

This script might come from a parent. It could come from news reports of corporate scandals. It could come from bitterness related to growing up in an impoverished environment. Several of our clients have witnessed their families disintegrating and relationships being destroyed as a result of what appeared initially to be good fortune when a relative won the lottery.

People who have internalized this script even twist evidence to support their belief. For example, some claim that the Bible says, "Money is the root of all evil." Actually, the verse they are quoting says that the *love* of money is the root of all evil. In other words, the Bible is saying that it isn't money that is the problem, but our relationship with money.

Our problematic relationship with money is not new and not just an American problem. The Bible offers insights about an appropriate relationship with money, in some form, more than two thousand times—more than any other single topic!

Regardless of the origin, people who live this particular money script have a hard time achieving financial success. They may unconsciously avoid hard work or opportunities for career advancement. The script becomes an excuse to rationalize poor job performance. Others may sabotage their success by making poor investment or business decisions.

The message becomes "If I avoid success and wealth, I won't be a bad person."

This money script, along with its variations, is one of the most common we see. Of course, people don't consciously sabotage their financial lives to remain poor. Instead, they unconsciously arrange their lives so that they can never accumulate a lot of money. Like the hapless football team that each week manages to "snatch defeat from the jaws of victory," these people continually find new ways to undermine their own success.

On the surface, this script seems obviously flawed or at least easily modified. However, we continue to be amazed at how such a simple belief can be so tightly held at an unconscious level . . . with disastrous consequences.

Consider Ernesto, who grew up on a plantation in Hawaii. His father, a foreman, held a position of authority. All the other kids on the plantation, children of the laborers, were of a different cultural heritage. In school, Ernesto was the "rich kid." He was ashamed that he had money because it meant that he was different. He often felt that the other kids resented his family's wealth. He was painfully aware of the financial struggles of his neighbors and classmates.

Ernesto, like all of us, just wanted to be accepted as a normal kid. He couldn't do anything about being different because of his cultural heritage, but he certainly could make sure he didn't set himself above anyone by having more money. Now in his early sixties, Ernesto sadly realizes that he has made a series of self-destructive financial decisions throughout his life. These decisions keep him from being able to retire, and he realizes now he will have to work for the rest of his life. None of this, of course, was decided on a conscious level. Ernesto held and acted on an unconscious belief that having money made him less desirable. Since he believed at some level that money was something he should be ashamed of, he made sure that he didn't accumulate any.

Of course, the opposite of this script is "Money is good." Indeed, money can bring peace and happiness into someone's life. However, Scrooge had lots of money, and it didn't bring him peace or happiness. We've had clients who were wealthy almost beyond comprehension, yet they weren't happy.

The truth is, money isn't "bad" or "good." Money just "is." It is a resource. It is inanimate. How we use it can be bad or good, but money itself is totally neutral.

2. "More money will make things better."

Another common money script is the belief that more money will solve most of life's problems. Unfortunately, it's not that easy.

There are dozens of variations of this money script. When that arbitrary "more money" point is reached, however, security or happiness never quite arrives. Instead, the "more money" point just moves a little farther out, much like the proverbial donkey chasing the carrot on a stick . . . always just out of reach.

> **When we get "more," the "enough"
> point moves farther away.**

This belief is often found among workaholics who believe that fulfillment and meaning will come together for them when they get just a little bit more. Sadly, it never seems to happen.

This money script may have been created at an early age when a child wanted a toy, a bicycle or the latest fashion. The parents told the child that they couldn't afford it. Perhaps the child saw other kids with fancy clothes or cars and thought that if only she had those clothes or cars she would be part of the "in" crowd, which would bring a sense of happiness and acceptance.

Of course, there are many others who hold the opposite belief: "Less is better." If they have little or no money, they feel somehow morally or spiritually superior to those that have money.

3. "I don't deserve money."

One variation of this script includes "I didn't work for this money, so I don't deserve it." Gene worked for a large company that required him and his family to move frequently. They made just enough to make ends meet and because of their frequent relocations, they never purchased a home. In Gene's family, money was something you never talked about. Gene's father was a poor farmer who was no stranger to hard manual labor. Gene's money script was that you don't deserve money not earned by hard labor. When Gene's father died, Gene was told his dad was in the process of selling the farm for $11,000,000. Because Gene and his father never talked about money, Gene had no idea of its value or that he would inherit the farm someday.

When Gene received the money from the sale of the farm, he put it in the bank and didn't touch it or the accumulating interest. One year after receiving the windfall he sought the help of a financial planner. He and his wife talked about their desire to someday own their own home. When the planner suggested that they had $11,000,000 in the bank and could easily afford a $200,000 house, the couple looked despondently at the floor. Using their inheritance was out of the question because they didn't deserve the money.

Another common variation of this money script is "Because so many are poor, I don't deserve to enjoy the money that I have." It's not unusual for a high-income person with this script to have relatively few assets. Why? They give away or spend their entire income because they unconsciously feel that they don't deserve to have money.

The flip side of the "I don't deserve money" script is "I *deserve* this." In this case, "this" is the individual's latest impulsive purchase. Entitlement—the belief that one deserves something—affects most overspenders or those who regularly bust their budgets.

4. "There will never be enough money."

Some people believe that there will never be enough money, so they live in a constant state of personal deprivation. This is common among the elderly who survived the Great Depression. These people find it difficult to spend on themselves even when the spending is critically important, such as for health or dental care.

The flip side of this script is "There will always be enough." Living this script guarantees that these people will never have enough, because once they accumulate even a little extra money, they spend it. Children of wealthy parents may be more at risk to internalize this money script. When all of one's wishes are easily met, it's easy to develop an unconscious belief that somehow the money will always be there, regardless of one's financial realities.

5. "Money is unimportant."

This script can arise from religious beliefs or simply by observing that many people who are wealthy aren't happy. It's also a relatively common belief among those who also believe that "money is bad."

This money script makes it easy to rationalize laziness, lack of ambition, poor financial planning, financial failure, or lack of focus or concern about financial matters.

In fact, some people might interpret our assertion that "it's not about money" as meaning that money is unimportant. We don't mean that at all. Life is about far more than money, but money still has an important place in it.

Money is a resource and as such, it's as important as other resources—good health, relationships, time, and our professional contacts and careers. We may need a little of all of these resources to reach our other, more important, life goals. And just as important as having these resources is our ability to manage them. Managing money as a resource is something about which Scrooge actually knew little.

Identifying Money Scripts

When we introduce the idea of money scripts to our clients, we get blank stares initially. Yet, after clients see a few examples, they can begin to identify some of their own money scripts. It's not uncommon for people to end up writing several pages worth of scripts in a twenty-minute period.

Everyone has money scripts. Once people start writing them down, they begin to bring their unconscious money scripts into conscious awareness. Becoming aware of money scripts is the first step to changing them and any related destructive behaviors.

**Money scripts are beliefs that are often
only partial truths about money.**

What Do You Believe About Money?

Word associations can offer clues about one's money scripts. The following exercise is a useful process to help people identify their belief patterns around money.

Exercise 1

WHAT ARE YOUR FIRST THOUGHTS ABOUT MONEY AND . . .

You'll need a pen and paper for this exercise. Write a statement describing what you think or believe about money in conjunction with each word or phrase listed below. Don't try to analyze your responses; just list them as quickly as possible. For example, a belief you have about money might be: "The rich . . . think differently than me." You may have several thoughts about money

and "the rich, "the poor," "politicians," etc. We encourage you to write down as many thoughts as you can for each the following words or phrases:

The rich	Spending	Budgets
The poor	Giving	College
Marriage	Financial advisers	Children
Your spouse	Taxes	Allowances
The church	Dying	Receiving
Work	Wills	Religion
Relatives	Borrowing	Banks
Happiness	Saving	Business
Retirement	Attorneys	Employers
Investing	Politicians	Employees
Food	Insurance	Love

Exercise 2

YOUR FIVE MOST DOMINANT MONEY SCRIPTS

Now, on your list, circle the five statements that you think are the most truthful or accurate, or the ones you have the strongest feelings about. These are your most dominant money scripts. We'll refer to these scripts later in the book, so it might be helpful if you take time to do this brief exercise now and write down your responses. This exercise alone has been life changing for some of our clients.

A participant in one of our workshops chose the following money scripts as his "Most True":

- The rich got that way by taking advantage of the poor.
- Getting ahead at work is all politics.
- I'll never be happy because I'll never have any money.
- Money is unimportant. Only family is important.
- The poor got that way because the rich take advantage of them.

These are the actual responses from a middle-aged man named Robert. Looking at this example, can you see any themes emerging? Given these money scripts, what might you predict are Robert's self-defeating money behaviors and their long-term consequences?

Robert is a nice enough guy, but you don't have to be a professional counselor to see that he is solidly locked into the role of being poor. He is and will continue to be unable to accumulate wealth even if a sudden money event occurs (an inheritance, lottery winning, insurance settlement, gift). It's easy to predict that he would probably get rid of the excess money in some self-defeating way because possessing wealth violates his basic unconscious beliefs about money, life and his self-image.

For example, saving for retirement is something Robert knew he ought to do, but never did. He didn't do it because as money accumulated he would be faced with the fact that his net worth in terms of money was increasing. Eventually, he would have had to acknowledge that he was becoming rich. His unconscious values could not permit this to happen. Even when his net worth, as judged by the net value of his business and property, indicated to others that he was wealthy, he adamantly denied that to be the case.

Sometimes, simply doing this exercise allows people to recognize their unconscious money scripts and begin to change them. It worked that way for Robert. After years of struggle and pain over self-defeating money behaviors, he suddenly saw the world differently. Once he became aware of his unconscious money scripts, he and his wife began saving aggressively for their retirement. Both professionals, they went from chronically undercharging for their services to receiving reasonable fees for their work. The changes were so immediate that it seemed miraculous to Robert, his family and his financial advisors.

Then there was Steve. After writing down more than sixty money scripts, he chose these as his top five:

- More money is better.
- Your net worth equals your self-worth.
- You have to work hard for money.
- Someday, the money will run out.
- Money will give me meaning in life.

What do you suspect Steve's behaviors around money are? If you guessed he is a driven, financially successful workaholic, you are right. Steve had no time for play, hobbies or relationships. Working and amassing wealth were his top priorities. Not surprisingly, Steve had suffered a broken marriage and had few friends. Unlike Robert, when Steve became aware of his money scripts, he didn't have a miraculous and immediate change in his destructive financial behaviors. He needed more than simple awareness.

Sometimes Awareness Isn't Enough

Regrettably, not all destructive money scripts and their associated behaviors are easily changed. Often, our most ingrained money scripts, those that drive our most chronic and destructive financial behaviors, can't be changed by simple awareness, sheer determination, effort or knowledge. These money scripts are held firmly in place by difficult emotions. They require a trip into our past. Unfortunately, few of us take that journey without prodding. For many of us, it takes an intervention, as it did for Scrooge.

Applying the Wisdom of This Chapter

1. Since children can't fully grasp adult reality, they translate what they see and hear into rules about money and life. These internalized messages are often only partial truths and are called *money scripts*. What are some of yours?

2. People are generally unaware of their money scripts and how their self-defeating behaviors are linked to those money scripts. What connections can you make between your money scripts and your money behaviors?

3. Which of your money scripts could be keeping you poor, unhappy and/or unfulfilled?

4. Like the broken clock that's accurate twice a day, even the most dysfunctional-sounding money scripts work . . . occasionally. Which of yours work some of the time—just often enough to reinforce that they are true?

5. Common money scripts include the following: "Money is bad." "More is better." "I don't deserve money." "There will never be enough." "Money is unimportant." What are some words you associate with money? Does the list sound like money is something positive? Negative? Neutral?

6. You can begin to identify your money scripts by using the exercises in this chapter. What are your top five money scripts? Based on their behaviors, what do you think are the top five money scripts of your closest friend? Mom? Dad? Partner?

2

MARLEY'S GHOST—

STAGE ONE: DENIAL AND INTERVENTION

Rarely easy, work with the soul is usually placed squarely in that place we would rather not visit, in the emotion we don't want to feel, and in that understanding we would prefer to do without.

—THOMAS MOORE
CARE OF THE SOUL

"You don't believe in me," observed the Ghost.
"I don't," said Scrooge.

—*A Christmas Carol*

Denial locks destructive money scripts in place. Denial is also a constant theme throughout *A Christmas Carol*.

At the beginning of the tale, Scrooge has no clue there is anything wrong with his behavior. His behavior matches his beliefs, and all seems right with his world—although he sees little right with the way everyone else conducts their lives. He is unable to see the incompleteness of his view about how the world works and what is important. He has not yet learned the First Principle of Financial Wisdom.

PRINCIPLE #1: DENIAL INHIBITS CHANGE

Scrooge's denial manifests itself in his lack of awareness about how money beliefs formed in his early childhood influence the quality of his adult life. Any discomfort that he feels merely reinforces his money script that "If I just had more money, things would be better."

Even before the visit from Marley's ghost, Scrooge is given three challenges to his denial, three chances to change his behavior. Each delivers, in its own way, a promise of a better life for him and others if Scrooge will just change his ways. Not only does Scrooge remain unchanged, he rebukes all three, illustrating the overwhelming strength of his money scripts.

The first challenge comes from Scrooge's nephew, Fred, who wishes Scrooge a Merry Christmas. Scrooge replies with some of the most famous words in nineteenth-century literature: "Bah! Humbug!"

Next, two churchwardens approach Scrooge for a donation to help the poor. "Are there no [debtor] prisons?" Scrooge mocks them. Dickens's own father wound up in debtors' prison twice, and young Dickens suffered mightily as a result, so he was well aware of the cruelness of Scrooge's response. Emotionally, his character Scrooge couldn't afford to open his heart or his wallet to the pain of the poor.

Finally, a caroler sings, "God bless ye, merry gentlemen," another symbolic reference to Scrooge being blessed if he changes his ways. Scrooge chases the caroler away with a ruler.

Christmas carols are, by definition and tradition, joyful songs of praise and thanksgiving. Carols represent the antithesis of Scrooge's personality at the start of the novel. When Scrooge chases away the caroler, he is symbolically denying joy and giving—the true spirit of Christmas.

Yet, Scrooge's behavior is perfectly understandable, given his beliefs. A positive response in any of these situations would violate at least one of Scrooge's money scripts. As these beliefs are so deeply held and emotionally charged, Scrooge is unable to accept any conflicting evidence that might suggest a more realistic and balanced view.

Modern-day versions of "nephews, wardens and carolers" come to us in many forms. Books and other media offer financial advice. Friends and personal advisors tell us that we need a will, that buying things with unsecured credit is not a good idea, that savings and retirement plans are essential. They may also advise us that constructing and following a spending plan can make life easier. They may warn us that we are crippling our children by financially bailing them out repeatedly or assure us that we have the talent, skill and opportunity to become even more successful. If our core belief systems, our money scripts, can't allow us to internalize messages such as these, then like Scrooge, we will ignore them and go on about our lives.

Sometimes everyday occurrences help us alter our money scripts. Most often, however, it takes more dramatic events. For Scrooge to break through his denial and begin to learn the principles of financial wisdom, it took the intervention of Marley's ghost.

Exercise 3

MODERN-DAY MESSAGES

Take a moment to list the three things you need to do or have been told you should do financially, but can't seem to make happen.

What would have to happen before you truly committed to making the changes?

The Intervention of Marley's Ghost

Marley's ghost provides the dramatic event needed to begin to shake Scrooge loose from his deeply ingrained money scripts. Ghosts have long been a staple of English literature. Shakespeare frequently used ghosts in his stories. Dickens, as a student of Shakespeare, obviously realized how well ghosts could be used to help move the plot in his stories. Marley's ghost, however, does more than move the plot along. Scrooge sees a glimpse of his own fate in the plight of his deceased business partner when Marley's apparition appears to Scrooge on Christmas Eve.

Marley's ghost is dragging a chain made of old ledgers, money boxes and other money trappings. To the reader, it's obvious that the chains Marley carries in death are symbols of the baggage from his past. They represent the very beliefs and behaviors that Scrooge still carries in life—things that will doom Scrooge to a similar afterlife unless he changes. Marley confirms to Scrooge that the chain that awaits him is already long and will be even longer, and that he is already dragging it around. But Scrooge is unable to see it. It's yet another example of the denial that keeps Scrooge from seeing the reality of his situation.

In spite of the appearance of this ghastly apparition and its dire warnings, Scrooge clings desperately to his crumbling denial, sarcastically joking that the apparition of Marley is more related to hallucinations caused by a bad meal than an actual experience:

> *"There is more of gravy than of the grave about you."*

Marley's ghost, doomed to wander the earth feeling the sorrow of others but unable to intervene, warns Scrooge that the same horrific fate awaits him. He further foretells that three ghosts will visit Scrooge. When Scrooge objects, Marley's ghost gives this prophetic reply:

> *"Without their visits, you cannot hope*
> *to shun the path I tread."*

Even so, Scrooge is terrified at the prospect of the visits of the spirits:

> *"I—think I'd rather not."*

Marley has provided a terrifying preview of what life will be like if Scrooge doesn't change, yet Scrooge still resists. Why?

Although Scrooge has been shown powerful reasons to change, he isn't quite ready. Intense emotions are often attached to money scripts. These powerful, unconscious emotions tie people to dysfunctional beliefs, even when their own logic tells them they should change.

Three Conditions Necessary for Change

Before people can change, however, three factors need to be present. First, a perception must exist that change is necessary. In other words, there must be enough pain or discomfort for us to realize that what we are doing is not working. Second, we must have some knowledge of what we need to do in order to change and the confidence that we can pull it off. Third, we must be ready and willing to do whatever is required to change.

Change is not made without inconvenience.
—Attributed to Richard Hooper, British Theologian;
as quoted by Samuel Johnson in the Preface to
the *Dictionary of the English Language, 1775*

Coauthor Rick Kahler lived in denial for many years, until a visit from his own Marley finally got his full attention.

Rick's Journey

BY RICK KAHLER, CFP*

Early in life I internalized at a very deep and unconscious level that real fulfillment comes with having money. My money scripts included "The more money you have, the happier you are," "Money will give you meaning" and "There will never be enough money."

Maybe that is why I identified from an early age with the story of Scrooge. It was my favorite Christmas story. I couldn't have told you why. In reality, Scrooge and I shared similar beliefs about money. As a child I was completely unaware of these money scripts.

Through the course of my life, I looked for fulfillment in a number of places. I had my church, a wife, friends and my work. One of the messages I internalized from my church was that having a lot of money was an outward sign that God was blessing your life. This fit right in with my unconscious money script that "The more money you have, the happier you are."

The one thing I hadn't experienced was having enough happiness, which I reasoned was because I didn't have enough money.

I remember as a teenager telling a friend that if I owned a house and had $10,000 in the bank, that would be enough. Within a few years, I owned the house and I had $10,000 in the bank. It then became laughable to me that I had been so naive. It wasn't enough. It was nowhere near enough!

I remember as a young adult thinking, "If I could accumulate $1,000,000 by my fortieth birthday, it would be enough." Well, I reached that goal. And it still wasn't enough. It wasn't even funny this time.

For most of my life, my well-being was directly related to my cash flow. In my early years of business, I was in real estate, a job that I hated as much as I loved. I became a fee-only certified financial planning practitioner (CFP®) in 1983, and I fell in love with the financial planning profession. Still, I didn't give up my day job as a Realtor. Real estate held a greater promise of accumulating wealth. I knew real estate, I was good at it. I had a system, and I was successful. At an unconscious level, I decided that the pursuit of the dollar was more important than being totally in love with my job because once I had enough money, I could do what I liked. I wasn't even aware that I was so busy working hard to accumulate wealth that I had no clue as to what "doing what I liked" might be.

In a few years, by the mid-80s, I had accumulated $1,000,000 worth of real estate. Then the economy slid into a recession. Mortgage interest rates skyrocketed to the midteens, house prices began a multiyear decline and tenants were scarce. My negative cash flow soared to $1,500 per month, which was more than a third of my total income. Looking at a balance statement became a paralyzing experience. My mortgage debt quickly exceeded my assets. My response was to put my nose to the grindstone. Refusing to look at the numbers and risk emotional paralysis, I worked as hard as I possible could to dig my way out. That survivalist state of mind continued to drive my behaviors for the next twenty years.

When my properties started to break even fifteen years later, I didn't even notice. I was so accustomed to working hard and not looking at the balance sheet and income statements, I was on autopilot.

During this time, my world began to unravel. While I financially struggled to keep all my businesses and real estate afloat, my own version of Marley came to visit me: my twelve-year marriage crumbled and I was alienated from my church, all in the same year. Discouraged and devastated, I had all the excuses in the world why I didn't need or want to look at my past. Fortunately, I sought out the guidance of a counselor and started my own journey.

Unlike Scrooge, my journey wasn't over in a night. For many years I journeyed with various counselors and experiential therapy groups. During that time, I thawed a lifetime of repressed emotions. Like Scrooge, I learned how to feel. I began to see how my unconscious money scripts were keeping me from seeing, hearing and living in the present.

Getting down to authenticity around who I am and what my life aspirations are is one of the most difficult things I've ever done in my life. Five years ago, I didn't have more than a foggy notion of what I loved in my life. Had you asked me what I would do on a day off, I couldn't have even answered the question—I was addicted to my work. At the same time, I liked only about 35 percent of my daily tasks. I was so immersed in this world that I wasn't aware of the incongruency, and it took me several years of working these exercises over and over to finally get clear. Now, you may say I am just slower than the average person, and that may be true. But my experience with my clients would suggest that I am not alone. A lot of us get pickled with the notion that "this is just the way it is."

Figuring out what it is you really love can be one of the hardest exercises you'll ever undertake as an adult. I know it was for me. And, like many of my clients, I suffered a lot of shame in figuring this out. "I should know this stuff!" I told myself over and over. Well, I didn't, and getting down to what is real didn't come quickly or easily.

As a result of applying the financial wisdom of Scrooge, I've stopped almost all my day-to-day involvement with the real estate business that was, financially speaking, my most successful endeavor. The business made my house payment and paid the bills. The problem was, it didn't feed my soul. I got up in the morning dreading the day. I didn't like the business and hadn't liked it for twenty years. But for most of my adult life it defined me and fed me, so I felt obligated to give it the bulk of my energy and time.

When I started to explore my own relationship with money, I became painfully aware of my dislike for my day job. Once, in a workshop, I was asked to respond to the following question: "If the doctor told you that you had five to seven years to live, how would you live your life?" Of the many things I wrote down, one of them was that I would sell my real estate business. That was my first conscious hint that maybe I needed an occupational shift. But even the thought of quitting evoked deep fear.

It has taken several years of conscious work to be in a place to let go of my daily involvement in that business. To do so, I've had to uncover many money scripts and feel the difficult emotions that held them in place. I've felt so many complicated feelings around these issues that I wondered if I would ever get through them. I have removed barriers that were sapping me of my authentic energy. Today, most of my energy is going where my passion is, which is integrated financial planning, speaking and writing.

In the first year of my transition from real estate to doing only financial planning, I made less money than I had in a long time. That, of course, was at the core of my fear. You may remember that two of my major money scripts were "The more money you have, the happier you are," and "There will never be enough money." While I was in transition from the old toward the new, I encountered more change and financial challenges than at any time in my life. Yet, to my own amazement and that of those close to me, I had never been more energized or happier. In the midst of this financial chaos and change, I also had never been more conscious or at peace.

Do I still have difficult emotions? Yes. Am I still discovering unconscious money scripts? Yes. Am I able to use new tools to work through those emotions and come to clarity, integrity and authenticity? Most of the time! And am I living in more abundance than at any other time in my life? Absolutely!

That's the payoff of listening to my Marley and following my ghostly guides. They showed me the future I was creating, and I was fortunate to have the opportunity to change it. I hope that same opportunity will be yours.

Okay, Okay, I'll Change. . . . But Make It Quick!

At the beginning of Marley's visit, Scrooge is in total denial about his need to change. By the end of the visit, however, he begins to realize that the way he is living his life is not working for him—at least he is frightened of the potential consequences—and knows he must endure the spirits' visits. However, like many of us who realize that we need to change, Scrooge wants to get it over with as quickly and as painlessly as possible. When Marley tells Scrooge that three separate ghosts will visit him, Scrooge counters:

"Couldn't I take 'em all at once and have it over?"

If only it were that easy. Although his attitude has improved a bit, Scrooge really isn't ready to change yet. One could guess that he might be having misgivings about his ability to alter his behavior at this late stage of his life. He hopes he can find a salvation that will only require him to change in an easier, gentler and subtler way.

Exercise 4
MONEY SCRIPT LOG

Another powerful method for identifying and exploring your money scripts—and possibly chipping away at denial—involves keeping a Money Script Log. Some people may have difficulty identifying money scripts without a here-and-now awareness of any uncomfortable feelings around money experiences. This adaptation of a cognitive-behavioral therapy tool allows you to examine your behaviors, feelings and unconscious thinking patterns around money throughout your day. It also gives you another way to rescript limiting money scripts or to identify adaptive money behaviors.

The first component of the log involves identifying a behavior or situation that causes you distress about your relationship with money. This might involve an action, such as a purchase, or a nonaction—e.g., not doing something you know you need to do, such as outlining a spending plan. You can identify that you are in distress when you have an uncomfortable feeling or body sensation related to your behaviors, when you feel guilt about a particular behavior or when you feel you have to keep secrets from loved ones concerning your money behaviors.

After identifying the specific behavior and accompanying physical sensation or emotions, you then ask yourself, "What is the possible message I am receiving from my body?" or "What money-related thought is going through my mind right now?" Once this is identified, take some time to consider your family history and the experiences that might have led to internalizing this message. What person, people, experience or experiences gave you this message? This is a money script.

Lastly, challenge yourself to identify some other truths that would make the money script more accurate or functional. We call this process rescripting, and we talk about it in more depth in chapter 4. For many of us, identifying alternative and more accurate money scripts can be a difficult step. We are so familiar with our ingrained money scripts that we accept them as a universal reality. If you find this step difficult, we suggest you ask the opinion of someone who has a relationship with money that is different from yours. Asking someone with the same limiting worldview as yours might serve to further ingrain an incomplete money script. You could also ask yourself this question: "What might my counselor/coach/financial planner/CPA say about this?"

The Money Script Log can be taken with you throughout the day to record your experiences as they are happening. Or you can work on it later in the day when you reflect on your experiences. This log enables you to identify money patterns and to challenge your limiting and/or inaccurate beliefs about money. The process can begin to give you a sense of peace in your relationship with money.

Some examples of Money Script Log entries are listed in the following table.

Behavior or Situation	Physical Sensation or Feeling	Possible Message	Money Script	Alternative Money Script and/or Adaptive Behavior
Spent $1,000 on business clothes.	Felt sick to stomach and guilty.	It is wrong to spend money on clothes.	I don't deserve nice things.	If it fits into my overall budget, I deserve to spend money on self-care. / Share feelings with partner who supported purchase. In my business, how one physically presents oneself is important.

Behavior or Situation	Physical Sensation or Feeling	Possible Message	Money Script	Alternative Money Script and/or Adaptive Behavior
I know I am spending too much money, but I avoid setting up a spending plan.	Muscle tension, fear, perhaps anger when my spouse brings up the topic.	If I have a budget, I will live in deprivation.	I work hard, so I deserve to have what I want.	If I follow a savings and spending plan, I can retire comfortably. / Buy a book on spending plans and begin next month.
My business deal just fell apart.	A knot in my stomach and unable to eat.	I am going to go broke.	The money will run out; there will never be enough.	Leading a life of abundance, authenticity and fulfillment is not about the money. I have enough money to live a rich and fulfilling life.

The Faces of Denial

Denial in and of itself is not always a bad thing. It has a place in helping us maintain our psychological welfare and assisting us in the initial stages of coping with situations that are overwhelming. For example, it is not unusual for those who have undergone significant physical or emotional trauma to experience a type of emotional and psychological anesthesia, or denial. This creates a feeling of detachment and makes remembering significant portions of the traumatic event difficult.

However, when an individual is not actually in physical or psychological danger, or when the danger has passed, denial can work against a person by numbing his or her experience of the world. The same mechanism that is unconsciously employed to aid in survival can later become a significant hindrance to one's growth.

Today, similar nonfunctional denial keeps millions poor, stops millions from achieving their goals and dreams, and impedes those who are fortunate enough to have money from enjoying true prosperity and abundance. Unconscious money scripts are threatening the futures, the retirements, the legacies and the lives of millions of people and their loved ones.

Like Scrooge, millions of people
are crippled by their denial.

Our unexamined money scripts have a way of keeping us financially, emotionally and spiritually poor in spite of how much or how little money we've accumulated. So . . . why don't we change? Why don't we just see the facts and change our behavior?

Knowing What Is Right Is Not Always Enough

Think of the people who surround you in your day-to-day life. Do you see people whose behaviors or lifestyles are self-destructive? Of course! It's hard *not* to see them once you look.

Just look around you. You'll see people destroying their bodies with chemical and behavioral addictions to nicotine, alcohol, recreational drugs, work, sex and, yes, even exercise. Others are sabotaging their health by undereating or overeating. Then there are people who destroy their finances by overspending, undersaving or just plain neglecting financial things. You'll see people making impulsive purchases, buying things they really don't need and probably can't afford. Most of these people *know* they should take steps to change. They *know* that their behaviors are compromising their quality of life, their health and their future. Yet they fail to take real steps toward change.

The late 1990s saw millions of intelligent and informed investors swept up in a stock market mania where they paid exorbitant sums of money for the shares of technology companies that had never made a profit. The aftermath found many losing 25 to 75 percent of their invested capital. Most of these investors knew better.

Sometimes, awareness or knowledge alone is not enough. When this is the case, we need intervention from an outside source: a traumatic event (such as a divorce, sudden death, the birth of triplets or a letter from the IRS), a counselor, a workshop. Perhaps, for some, reading this book may provide the necessary intervention.

Some of our clients realize they should be spending less or not working so much. They know they should save more, worry less, draw up a will, stop bailing their adult children out of financial crises and so on. Even when they know—they *know!*—that they're acting irrationally, they feel powerless to change their behavior. The reason? They just aren't emotionally ready to change.

Mark and Theresa, for example, have two children from their current marriage and each has a child from a previous marriage. Mark owns a successful business. Theresa is an accomplished professional. They have no will, which means they have named no guardian for their children and stepchildren. They would tell you that they definitely don't want the state deciding how their family should be split up. Still, although they know they need a will, it's just too painful to discuss.

Is there a simple solution?

Yes. A will.

Is the solution simple?

No.

When we know we need to change but are unable to do so, the first stop on our journey to a new future is a visit to explore our past.

Applying the Wisdom of This Chapter

1. What are the financial issues that your denial keeps you from taking action on? What things do you know you should do that you just can't seem to get around to doing?

2. If you were to look closely at one of those issues, would you say you just aren't ready? Or that you lack the confidence to accomplish the task, and just don't know how to start? Or that you don't really think it is that big a deal?

3. Have you tried to act on one or more of these issues and failed, just couldn't seem to make it happen? Are you aware of any old messages you have internalized that make it difficult for you to be successful?

3

THE FIRST OF THE THREE SPIRITS—

STAGE TWO: EXPLORING THE PAST

The heritage of the past is the seed that brings forth the harvest of the future.

—NATIONAL ARCHIVES BUILDING,
WASHINGTON, D.C.

"Who and what are you?" Scrooge demanded.

"I am the Ghost of Christmas Past."

"Long past?" inquired Scrooge.

"No. *Your* past."

—*A Christmas Carol*

At this point, some readers may lament, "Do I really have to look into the past? I've tried so hard to put the past behind me! Can't I just skip this part? Why dwell on the past?"

Besides, isn't looking back the opposite of what we've been taught to do all our lives? Shouldn't we be looking forward to the future? Why not just keep the past behind us and lock it away? After all, it's "water under the bridge," isn't it? Even professional advisor and counselor communities are conflicted about the need to ever look back to move forward.

Granted, sometimes it's not always necessary. We frequently see clients who are getting by in spite of their destructive behaviors around money. We suspect that one reason some of you may be reading this book is that you are tired of just getting by.

The challenge comes when people realize that a specific money belief is sabotaging their goals and plans, and that awareness is not enough to help them change their behavior.

When this happens, there is usually a difficult emotion that is linked to a past event or series of events that keeps the dysfunctional money script locked in place. Thus, the self-defeating behavior continues. It is often the unconscious fear of feeling the pain from these emotions that keeps one from changing. Typically, as in the case of Scrooge, to begin to unlock and feel these emotions requires a visit to the past.

Still, you may be thinking, "Let sleeping dogs lie." Scrooge was no different. He was terrified of looking into his past.

Fear of the Light

The Ghost of Christmas Past is a frightening sight:

> *"Being now a thing with one arm, now with one leg, now with 20 legs, now a pair of legs without a head, now a head without a body. . . ."*

In spite of this ghastly sight, Scrooge is most distressed by a bright jet of light that springs from the ghost's head, obviously a symbol for illumination of the past. Scrooge begs the ghost to cover the light. The ghost refuses:

> *"Would you so soon put out the light I give?*
> *Is it not enough that you . . . forced me through years*
> *to wear [this cap to hide the light] low upon my brow!"*

Scrooge's seemingly irrational fear of the light symbolizes his unconscious fear of the truth that is locked in his past and the accompanying emotions he has locked away so carefully.

When the ghost gently takes his arm and heads for the window, Scrooge is so afraid that he fears he might die:

> *"I am mortal," Scrooge objected, "and likely to fall."*

One of our clients, Bob, recently told us about starting his journey to discovery:

> "It took a tremendous leap of faith to embark on my journey of discovery. I would liken my experience to what I have read about those who talk of near-death experiences, the Christ story or the rising of the phoenix. I know this sounds dramatic, but it was like that for me. Before starting the journey—and sometimes now, after I am well into the journey—I felt like I had jumped on a fast moving train having no clue of the destination. Whether I consciously made the jump or not, I knew intuitively I was headed somewhere, my life was about to change and I was not the engineer but along for the ride. It was, and is, the journey of a lifetime, the most important trip I have ever taken and perhaps the only one that is genuinely mine. A trip to under-standing and accepting who I am totally."

Despite Scrooge's trepidation, his travels with the Ghost of Christmas Past will take him back to early scenes of his childhood and teenage years. There, he will begin to experience some of the difficult feelings associated with some of those painful events for the first time in decades. As with Scrooge, this potentially scary journey to our past is often made easier and safer with a guide.

FINANCIAL THERAPISTS

Amazingly, the behaviors of the three ghosts visiting Scrooge are very similar to those of today's financial counselors. Of course, Dickens couldn't have known that. Therapy of any kind, let alone financial therapy, didn't exist in Victorian England. Financial therapy is still rare today. Dickens must have been truly inspired to capture these universal truths about life in the six weeks it took to write the entire book!

Ghost as Counselor

When Scrooge is fearful of taking the first steps into his past, the spirit reassures him:

> *"Bear but a touch of my hand [on your heart]," said the spirit,*
> *"and you shall be upheld in more than this!"*

Like a good counselor, the Ghost of Christmas Past is nonjudgmental, nonshaming and compassionate as it guides Scrooge into his forgotten past. The spirit visits each scene just long enough for Scrooge to get in touch with, and express, his long-repressed feelings. In some cases these feelings involve intense joy; in other cases they involve deep grief and sorrow. Once the lesson had been learned, and the long-repressed feelings allowed expression, the spirit moves Scrooge on to the next event, even when Scrooge begs to linger at times.

CAROL TRIVIA

The nondirective, noninterpretational approach of the Ghost of Christmas Past is similar to the humanistic counseling approach advocated by Carl Rogers and other modern psychologists.

Driven by His Past

The first place the ghost takes Scrooge is to his childhood home. As Scrooge remembers this place, his feelings seem overwhelming:

> *"He was conscious of a thousand odours floating*
> *in the air, each one connected with a thousand thoughts,*
> *and hopes, and joys, and cares long, long, forgotten!"*

The ghost merely assists Scrooge in opening doors to view his past. The spirit provides no interpretation of what Scrooge sees and experiences. Analysis and commentary aren't necessary. From the perspective of an adult, Scrooge begins to understand how the feelings of his childhood are connected to his current behaviors. However, the act of remembering long-forgotten events can sometimes trigger other painful memories and feelings. As Scrooge relives the traumatic events of his past, his pain is immediate.

CAROL TRIVIA

Dickens writes that odors can actually trigger long-forgotten memories. It will take another century before modern psychology begins to grasp a full understanding of this process.

As we travel with Scrooge through his past, we learn that he has had more than his share of difficult experiences and memories. Getting in touch with these memories and the emotions attached to them is a major step in unlocking the door of the prison created by his self-defeating money scripts. Viewing the touching scenes from his childhood, Scrooge begins to feel the sadness that has been buried for decades. As he feels this sadness, tears fill his eyes:

> *"Your lip is trembling," said the Ghost.*
> *"And what is that upon your cheek?"*

As the tears fall, Scrooge begins the healing process, feeling and releasing the heavy load of grief and sadness he has been carrying for all those years.

As we visit each memory, Dickens provides clues as to why Scrooge is the way he is.

Young Scrooge was apparently treated so badly by his father that he was afraid to come home for the holidays and stayed at his boarding school alone. Abandoned and insecure, young Scrooge learned to distrust others and apparently had

---

CAROL TRIVIA

Young Scrooge turns to the great novels for companionship. One positive effect was Scrooge's education, which led to his business success.

---

a hard time making friends. His sister, as seen in Christmas Past, tells young Scrooge it is safe to come home:

"Come [home]. Father is so much kinder than he used to be."

Young Scrooge's defensive distrust of people may have been the foundation of his money script "Don't trust others with your money." As a child, Scrooge didn't have the ability to defend himself, so the only option he could see was to distance himself from others. If he didn't get close to others, he wouldn't get hurt.

While this adaptation protected him as a child, the same defense mechanism had a profoundly negative effect on the adult Scrooge. He grows up to believe that relationships with others have little to offer except pain. He believes that trusting or loving someone will only result in more hurt. Young Scrooge rejected his childhood sweetheart because she came from a poor family. Even as a young man, Scrooge had already placed the pursuit of money above love. In this touching scene, his betrothed leaves him because he cannot see beyond his money scripts:

"You fear the world too much," she answered gently. "I have seen your nobler aspirations fall off one by one, until the master passion

*Gain, engrosses you.... Even if you were free today, can I even believe you
would choose a dowerless girl? ... I release you with
a full heart, for the love of him you once were."*

Scrooge chooses to abandon love, and with it, the love of
his life. The adult Scrooge has only one friend, his business
partner, Marley. He places little value on friendship that is
outside of a business relationship and believes, instead, that
"Money will give meaning to my life." This money script
causes Scrooge to miss one of humanity's greatest sources of
happiness: close and intimate relationships with other
human beings.

Scorned by his father and with no friends at school, young
Scrooge grows up to believe that money is the answer—if he
can just earn enough of it.

Unfortunately, "Money will give meaning to my life" and
some of Scrooge's other money scripts—"Don't spend
money on yourself or others" ... "You can never have enough
money" ... "If I had more money, things would be better"—
were at the core of many of his destructive behaviors and
drove Scrooge to hoard every penny.

Some things never change. We see similar money scripts
lived out today with the same results that Scrooge experienced.

Exercise 5

COUNTING YOUR LOSSES

As our clients move through their history, they often begin to feel the full impact of their life experiences for the first time, including the lost opportunities and destroyed relationships. Can you relate any of the painful experiences of your adult life to adaptations you made to your painful childhood experiences? Possible examples include: spending time working while missing too many of your children's once-in-a-lifetime growing-up experiences; not speaking up for yourself because you learned as a child it was better to be quiet than cause a fuss; overindulging your children because you grew up feeling deprived.

Fezziwig's Ball

Up to this point in the story, all the scenes from Scrooge's life pass quickly—but not before Scrooge accesses a wealth of forgotten feelings around each of them. The ghost moves on immediately when Scrooge has seen and felt enough.

Fezziwig's Christmas ball is a notable exception to Scrooge's rapid journey through the past. Young Scrooge was an apprentice under a rich merchant named Fezziwig, who threw a large gala every Christmas. The joyous occasion is described in great detail, as is Fezziwig's irrepressible enthusiasm. The Ghost of Christmas Past gives Scrooge ample time to enjoy this happy festival from his past.

Instead of seeing Fezziwig's life as a model of joy, celebration and sharing one's wealth and good fortune freely, young Scrooge's early experiences cloud his vision. Indeed, they may have implanted an erroneous, yet powerful, belief that will eventually become Scrooge's most tragic money script:

> *"If I had more money, then things would be better."*

After internalizing this belief, young Scrooge becomes obsessed with accumulating money and fearful of wasting even a shilling. He loses sight of the true reason he wanted to be rich in the first place, to feel joy and happiness. Scrooge was so focused on hoarding money that he never learned to *enjoy* the fruits of his labor.

For Lasting Change, Start with Your Past

The answer to how we can change our most ingrained money scripts often lies in the past. That's where we must look, regardless of how dark or frightening our trip into the past might seem to be.

**Your feelings about the past cannot hurt you,
but they *can* imprison you.**

Unless we are able to feel the pain that surrounds our strongest money scripts, we won't be able to permanently alter our behaviors. Without dissipating the difficult emotions that hold them in place, we will keep grabbing the same old scripts again and again, sabotaging every attempt to reach success, happiness and financial freedom.

PRINCIPLE #2: TO HEAL YOU MUST FEEL

Feeling and expressing old, pent-up emotions allows our senses to reawaken and enables us to take in new information. Our senses provide us with the opportunity to see and experience what is happening around us. If there has been a pattern of unresolved historic financial trauma or painful experiences we have not processed, we may have shut down the full effect of our sensory systems. Recalling these memories can enable us to be more fully present for what is happening around us today. In some ways feelings are all or nothing—for example, if you don't allow yourself to feel sadness, you can't fully experience joy.

The good news is that when we begin to identify the source of our money scripts and become open to feeling the emotions

---

ENLIGHTENMENT

We see similar moments of enlightenment in our work. Once individuals begin reawakening their feelings around past hurts, they can see more clearly how their perception of the past is impacting their actions today. In that magic moment, they begin to change.

surrounding them, we can start to see the world differently, more clearly. Money scripts stripped of the difficult and unfelt emotions that hold them in place no longer have power over us.

Once you feel it, you can heal it!

When we separate the feelings from the memory and the resulting thought—or belief—we begin the healing process. Repressed or pent-up emotions are released, and we are able to see things as they really are. Clarity and objectivity are the payoff for feeling our difficult emotions. What an incredible experience this can be! Once we're no longer bound by the limitations of these stubborn powerful money scripts, we can modify those scripts to better serve us in the future.

Feeling our repressed emotions around dysfunctional money scripts allows us to change our current behaviors in a lasting way.

The next story, by one of this book's coauthors, illustrates this process.

Nothing to Wear
BY TED KLONTZ, PH.D.

"You don't have anything right to wear," said a friend of mine, more serious than not. "Here's what I want you to do. Go to a good clothing store and tell them where you are going, how long you are going to be there and who you will be working with. Then just do what they tell you. No questions or arguments from you. Just do it."

He had just invited my wife and me to Manhattan for a long weekend to conduct a workshop for high-profile couples from the New York area.

I did as he directed and two weeks later walked out of the store with over $2,000 in receipts for three days' worth of "dress-up" clothes. As I got to the car, my head started pounding, I felt sick to my stomach and I actually thought for a moment I might pass out. A seizure, a heart attack, low blood pressure? Nothing that dramatic. Even as these physical sensations were going through my body, I knew it had to do with buying those new clothes. I had never spent so much money on clothes for myself at one time in my life, and I literally felt sick about it. I knew it was about spending the money, a lot of money, on myself, for clothes. I am a blue jeans kind of guy.

It wasn't logical and didn't make any economic sense to be concerned about this purchase. My friend, the sponsor of the program, had built the cost of my new wardrobe into our fees, so it wasn't about the money.

I have always been willing, even eager, to spend money on other people if I thought it would make them happy. But I never felt comfortable buying anything for myself except for the bare necessities. Buying blue jeans and some shirts every few years was about the extent of my clothing forays. I still have, and wear on a daily basis, clothes I've had for fifteen years. In fact, the only suit I had was purchased over twenty years ago. The most I had ever spent on clothes for myself at one time was maybe $150, and that had been only once or twice.

I was scheduled to go back and pick up the altered clothes a week later. When I got to the store's parking lot, I literally couldn't get out of the car, although the clothes were already paid for. I was paralyzed. I just sat in my car in the parking lot. I finally left after sitting there for ten minutes. I had to have my wife come back to the store with me later to get my clothes.

Though I would later joke about and tell this story many times, I truly couldn't understand why I felt and behaved that way. Knowing that the behavior was silly and strange didn't change it or make it better for me. I knew that it had to do with some deep belief—a money script that I was carrying around about money, clothes and myself— but I didn't know what to do about changing it.

It would be two years later, when I was conducting a workshop and using as examples statements my grandfather had made to me fifty years earlier, that I suddenly remembered hearing over and over as a kid, "You should feel fortunate to have something to eat, a roof over your head and anything to wear."

As the words, "You should feel lucky to have something to wear, lucky to have anything to wear, clothes, lucky, you should feel . . ." continued to go around in my mind, I felt a deep pang of sadness, hurt and loneliness. These were feelings I must have had when I asked for something as a kid and was given the mantra "You should feel lucky," or, in other words, "You should not want." As I allowed these words a hearing in my mind and felt the long-repressed emotions around them, I felt something shift inside me. I knew intuitively, without a doubt, that this ancient, well-ingrained, childhood message had been the source of my dis-ease in not only buying clothes for myself, but also for my more general discomfort in doing/wanting anything for myself.

The dance my wife and I had played for decades was "What do you want for your birthday, Christmas, to do, go, to eat, etc.?" "I don't know. I can't think of anything really," was my honest response. When she, or anyone else, would ask me a question like that, my mind would go blank. For years I jokingly called that my "birthday white-out." I have since discovered that I am not the only one who suffers from this phenomenon. I know it drove my wife nuts, because rather than take me at my word and get or do nothing, she would eventually have to guess, and do something. Then she would sense my general disappointment when the special day or moment came—disappointment because unconsciously I wanted something and didn't get it. Though my wife has many talents, mind reading isn't one of them.

That awareness was followed by another. I became aware of a long-standing money script in my family that to want or ask for anything specific was to appear ungrateful and selfish. Especially selfish. To be a good person in my clan, you were not supposed to actually tell someone what you wanted when they asked. So over the years, I gradually lost touch with wanting anything.

Recalling this memory also helped me understand the incongruity of my behavior around gifts. While being frugal with myself, I had a compulsive generosity when it came to giving to others, often to excess. I now understand that I was trying to protect others, especially my family, from those painful feelings I had as a kid growing up.

Visiting Your Past

In Scrooge's case, looking into the past was instantaneous. He merely took the ghost's hand and poof! He was witnessing each past event as if he were actually there.

For us, it's not quite as easy. On the other hand, most of us would not want to leap out a second-story window hand-in-hand with a ghost as Scrooge did! Thankfully, that is not our only option. Over the last hundred years, modern psychology has developed many approaches to help people go back into their past safely and bring insight and healing to otherwise difficult or traumatic memories.

There are many methods we use to assist clients in working through unfinished business from the past. Merely acknowledging and talking about the memories, with openness to experiencing whatever emotions arise, can be incredibly healing.

When the historic problem involves a relationship, some counselors will assist the client in addressing the unresolved issues directly with that person in a safe and mutually beneficial way. Others will encourage the use of visualization, meditation, role-playing and/or journaling to help clients get in touch with and process unresolved thoughts and emotions.

While we employ all these methods, we also use an additional tool we find incredibly effective: psychodramatic re-enactment. Using music, art, movement, role-playing and /or therapeutic sculpting, we assist clients in re-creating, symbolically, significant relationships, financial circumstances or events that they identify as needing to revisit. This experience is like being caught up in a great movie or book; the scenes can become very lifelike. The "then and there" quickly become the "here and now," as they did for Scrooge.

Many of these scenes represent times and places where the client felt vulnerable and disempowered. With a therapeutic guide, clients are given the opportunity to follow their hearts and do what they needed to do, say what they needed to say and feel what they needed to feel to heal. Often, previously repressed feelings of anger, sadness and joy are released and new understandings and insights are achieved.

The release of these feelings and the gaining of new understanding are empowering, cathartic, clarifying experiences. Like Scrooge, clients are motivated as never before to begin making changes.

If you'd like to know more about the psychodramatic re-enactment style of counseling, visit *www.wisdomofscrooge.com*. We've seen people make profound and lasting changes in their lives using this process, which is strikingly similar to that used by Dickens . . . without the ghosts, of course!

Carol Trivia

Did Dickens anticipate modern psychology? Fifty years after Dickens wrote *A Christmas Carol,* Sigmund Freud would write about repressed childhood memories. Freud observed how Dickens's own childhood provided inspiration for the plot in *Great Expectations.* Freud even wrote about the gallows laughter employed in Dickens's novels. Was the Father of Psychology influenced by Charles Dickens?

The Journey Can Be Difficult

The ability to look into the past varies with each individual. Some find it relatively easy to do. Others approach it with the same dread as Scrooge. Even with the ghost's support, Scrooge eventually is overwhelmed by his traumatic past. He begs to end the session:

> *"Spirit!" said Scrooge in a broken voice,*
> *"Remove me from this place!" "I cannot bear it!"*

The spirit reminds Scrooge that the scenes and feelings were not created by the ghost, but were actually a part of Scrooge's life:

> *"They are what they are."*

Scrooge finally can take no more. He grabs the spirit's candlesnuffer and pulls it over its head until it eventually covers the spirit's entire body.

> *"But though Scrooge pressed it down with all his force,*
> *he could not hide the light; which streamed from under it,*
> *in an unbroken flood upon the ground."*

The message? Awareness, once gained, cannot be easily extinguished.

Going into the past requires courage, faith, persistence, help and support. It is not a journey for the faint of heart or those who are not determined to change their course in life. It can be an exhausting experience.

Still, the payoff can be spectacular. With the past no longer ruling our lives, we can travel into the present and experience abundance, authenticity and clarity.

For Scrooge, the present comes in the form of the next nocturnal visitor—the Ghost of Christmas Present.

Applying the Wisdom of This Chapter

1. As best you can, recall the memorable experiences you have had with money, both good and painful. Go as far back in your memory as you can. We have our clients actually draw a picture or a symbol to represent each memory.

2. Go back and put a feeling word next to each of the items. Use words like angry, sad, happy, afraid, hurt.

3. Now look over everything you have written and ask yourself: "Looking at everything that has happened, if I had to write one or two sentences to summarize my experiences with money, what would they be?" Another way to do this would be to finish this sentence: "The moral of my story is . . ."

4

THE SECOND OF THE THREE SPIRITS—

STAGE THREE: UNDERSTANDING THE PRESENT

*The present moment
is the only one over which
we have dominion.*

—THICH NHAT HANH

❦❧

Scrooge, not surprisingly, anxiously awaits the arrival of the Ghost of Christmas Present. When it does not arrive precisely as the clock strikes one, Scrooge is overcome with terror. He waits in fear for a quarter of an hour, trembling violently, before he notices a stream of light shining from under the door:

". . . which, being only light, was more alarming than a dozen ghosts."

Although Scrooge is even more frightened than with the appearance of the first ghost, he has already begun to sense the benefit of his visitors.

Curious, Scrooge gets up and opens the door. His dismal room has been transformed into a dazzling display of bounty. The Ghost of Christmas Present sits on a throne of Christmas plenty: turkeys, geese, mince pies, plum puddings and more. The ghost is holding a torch that illuminates the room. Its light symbolizes the enlightenment that Scrooge will soon experience.

Previously, Scrooge feared this enlightenment. He had even tried to extinguish the light coming out of the head of the Ghost of Christmas Past. This time, Scrooge seeks out the light instead of trying to extinguish it. He is ready for the next step in his transformation to wisdom.

For Dickens, the Ghost of Christmas Present represents abundance, authenticity and clarity. These qualities are in sharp contrast to the life Scrooge knew and lived.

Abundance

While we can assume Scrooge had enough money to live in abundance, he chose a life of poverty. His money script "Don't spend money on yourself or others" was so powerful that Scrooge was uncomfortable just being in the presence of such abundance. The ghost has to implore Scrooge to come closer and look at him:

"I am the Ghost of Christmas Present. Look upon me!"

Scrooge's fear and shame are so great that he can't look the Ghost of Christmas Present in the eye, and he hangs his head when the ghost addresses him. This may surprise many people, who would hold that Scrooge was proudly selfish. We would suggest that old Scrooge was self-*less*; that is, he had no sense of self or self-worth. In spite of his wealth, not only was spending money on himself not acceptable, doing so was a source of shame.

Fortunately for Scrooge, he was in the middle of the process of eliminating his shame and thereby elevating his self-worth. As we see with our clients, one of the benefits to Scrooge's going back to look at his childhood issues was that he was able to recognize the vulnerability and innocence of that little boy. When this occurs, the shame of his not being good enough begins to fade and self-compassion begins to emerge. He has visited the past, reexperienced his pent-up emotional pain and let go of the difficult emotions that kept his most entrenched money scripts in place. He has begun to reawaken his senses. He is now in a state of readiness to get on with the task of understanding the present, to begin gathering new information about what it means to live his life more authentically and abundantly. He humbly asks this spirit to

"Conduct me where you will. I went forth last night on compulsion,
and I learnt a lesson which is working now. To-night,
if you have aught to teach me, let me profit by it."

Authenticity

Authenticity is being who we really are. It is when our outsides match our insides, when our behaviors match our deepest core values and life aspirations. The Ghost of Christmas Present was a model of authenticity.

Dickens tells us that the ghost sits barefoot on an unadorned throne in simple clothes in spite of being surrounded by such abundance. The ghost is indifferent to fashion, shoes or material possessions—a clear statement about the unimportance of material things. His chest is exposed—a metaphor for transparency and openness:

> *"[His] breast was bare, as if disdaining*
> *to be warded or concealed by any artifice."*

Aligning our day-to-day life to reflect our core values, deepest desires and life aspirations is not an easy task. While Scrooge was able to do this in one night, for many of us the process can take years. Discovering who we are, at our deepest level, is often the most difficult, yet most rewarding, work we can do. Just as old Scrooge became a model of authenticity, so can we.

Clarity

The Ghost of Christmas Present asks and Scrooge agrees to enter and come closer to "know me better, man," highlighting Scrooge's readiness to see the world as it is. The ghost challenges Scrooge to see the present clearly, accurately and knowledgeably. This happens as Scrooge begins to obtain the knowledge he was lacking to effectively change and modify his money scripts.

Dickens describes the Ghost of Christmas Present and Scrooge as opposites of each other. In effect, the ghost represents the person that Scrooge can become:

- The ghost lives in abundance; Scrooge lives in poverty.
- The ghost models authenticity; Scrooge lives without knowing who he truly is.
- The ghost is clear and objective; Scrooge has been delusional and judgmental.
- The ghost lives in the present; Scrooge has been employing outdated and unnecessary survival adaptations he learned in his past and focusing on a vague, ill-defined sense of a future that drives his daily behaviors.

The pain Scrooge has been carrying from the past has completely concealed who he really is, not only from those around him, but more important, from himself. Scrooge knows nothing about authenticity, abundance or clarity. He hasn't been living his life in the present. The spirit, knowing this, rhetorically asks Scrooge if he has "ever seen the like of me before." Scrooge's answer is short, complete and clear:

"Never."

Scrooge has no concept of how the world could be any different from the way he has perceived it all his life.

Many people share Scrooge's attitude today. Successful as well as unsuccessful people have their own limited perceptions about how their current situations could be different. This is often the case when we can't see the present objectively or clearly. But once we have visited the past, experienced our old, unfelt feelings and processed the difficult emotions that hold our most entrenched money scripts in place, we are able to change. In a figurative, and sometimes even literal, way we can see, hear and feel with a degree of clarity never experienced before—even when we've already heard or thought about these feelings, ideas and incidents.

We can begin to experience the abundance of the present, live more authentically and gain the knowledge that will help modify or change our beliefs about money. Being fully present allows us to answer these questions:

- Who am I?
- How do others view me?
- What do I really want?
- How do I get there?
- What do I need to know?
- What do I need to do?

Sometimes the answers to these questions can hurt. Just as embracing the past can be painful, so also can a full awareness of the present. Let's face it, life isn't always joyful nor should it be. Perpetual and unrelenting joy without pain is impossible and is often a form of denial.

In addition to showing Scrooge the joy around him, the Ghost of Christmas Present also shows Scrooge how those closest to him experience him:

> "'The Founder of the Feast indeed!' cried Mrs. Cratchit, reddening.
> 'I wish I had him here. I'd give him a piece of my mind
> to feast upon, and I hope he'd have a good appetite for it.'

'My dear,' said Bob, 'the children! Christmas Day.'
'It should be Christmas Day, I am sure,' said she, 'on which one drinks the
health of such an odious, stingy, hard, unfeeling man as Mr. Scrooge.'"

"'He's a comical old fellow,' said Scrooge's nephew, 'that's the truth: and not
so pleasant as he might be. However, his offences carry their
own punishment . . . His wealth is of no use to him. He don't do any good
with it. He don't make himself comfortable with it. . . .'
'I have no patience with him,' observed Scrooge's niece. Scrooge's niece's
sisters, and all the other ladies, expressed the same opinion."

Ouch! Who wants to be present for that? But that type of
honest response is exactly what we need to learn, change and
grow. In addition to seeing the joy around him, the clarity
Scrooge received from his work in the past allows him to
actually hear, perhaps for the very first time, comments about
himself from others. While initially a painful experience,
Scrooge will use this information to better himself and, ulti-
mately, his world.

Scrooge's journey through the past has opened him up to
see the present with clarity, as it truly is.

Scrooge Views the World Differently

As soon as Scrooge begins to see his words and actions
for what they are, he wants to correct some of his poor

behaviors. He says quietly to the ghost:

"There was a boy singing a Christmas carol at my door last night. I should like to have given him something: that's all."

What has shifted in Scrooge? His visit to the past has reawakened his senses. He is able see his encounter with the caroler in a different light. He wishes he had responded differently, now that he is able to view his interaction more clearly.

Scrooge's trip to his past has cleared the path for him to take in new information, but just feeling his difficult emotions doesn't give him any new information. That is the job of the Ghost of Christmas Present—to give Scrooge the new information with which he can modify his destructive money scripts to fit his current situation. For the first time in his adult life, Scrooge is beginning to experience reality.

The ghost takes him to several locations to see others who are living in abundance and authenticity, despite harsh circumstances and a lack of money. Scrooge learns that regardless of money or situation, people can be happy. He learns that having money or not having money does not create happiness or misery. If these "less fortunate" souls (as Scrooge would have originally judged them) could celebrate life, why couldn't he?

Scrooge sees:

• A Christmas celebration in a lonely lighthouse.
• Sailors humming Christmas carols to themselves though

trapped onboard their ship in miserable weather.

- A poor family living in a mud hut joyfully singing carols.
- The Cratchits enjoying a festive Christmas dinner.
- His nephew, Fred, hosting a joyous Christmas party, a party to which Scrooge was invited but replied, "Bah! Humbug!"

At each new venue, people are enjoying themselves, laughing and savoring the moment—something Scrooge has forgotten how to do; something he thought only having a lot of money could produce.

Scrooge considers, for the first time, that it just might be possible to be happy without money. This is a profound shift in his thinking. Do you remember his money scripts around happiness?

- Money will give you meaning in life.
- The more money you have, the happier you will be.
- You can never be happy if you are poor.

His encounters with the Ghosts of the Past and the Present have helped Scrooge begin to modify and change these money scripts. Scrooge is able to see that all the following are also true:

- People can be rich and happy.
- People can be poor and happy.
- People can be poor and miserable.
- People can be rich and miserable.

Scrooge is learning the power of the next principle of financial wisdom.

PRINCIPLE #3: IT PAYS TO BE PRESENT

Modifying Money Scripts

We become present when we are able to see the world clearly, live authentically and experience abundance. We can do this only when we change or modify our destructive money scripts and their associated behaviors. To change our most deeply ingrained money scripts, we first need an intervention that will challenge our distorted thinking. As we've discovered, Marley was Scrooge's intervention.

Next, we need to break the denial. This requires a visit from our own personal Ghost of Christmas Past to help us recall, identify and dissipate the difficult emotions that hold our denial of them in place. Not every destructive money script is deeply ingrained, however, or held in place by a difficult emotion. In fact, modifying some money scripts only takes becoming aware of how the script no longer serves us.

Next, regardless of how strong a money script is, we need new information about what money is and how it works to modify or change the script. That information can come to us in two ways: through instruction or observation.

When We Are Ready to Hear

First, let's consider instruction. Scrooge was clueless about what he needed to learn. Fortunately, he had the Ghost of Christmas Present to guide and teach him. Likewise, we need guidance and instruction to create abundance and authenticity in our lives. When we awaken to the present, there is much for most of us to learn about how to create financial abundance. This is the time when many of us will be ready and able to absorb more knowledge about how to modify our money scripts and start creating abundance in our life. It is as if the blinders have dropped from our eyes and the earplugs have fallen from our ears.

Abundance can take many forms, including mental, spiritual, physical and financial. Let's focus for a moment on financial abundance. Now, this is when reading a good book on financial planning or attending a financial workshop can pay big dividends. Having let go of difficult emotions from the past and brought our self-defeating money scripts into awareness, we are able, finally, to actually hear new information.

We can also learn by observing people who model healthy behavior. Both Fred and Fezziwig modeled being present in the world. Both lived in abundance with what they had and what they could reasonably afford. Both were authentic; their internal values matched their external behaviors. Both were clear and objective. The difference was that Fred was poor, at least by Scrooge's standards, and Fezziwig was rich. When the ghost showed Scrooge these models, Scrooge was able to see examples of what a more balanced relationship with money looked like.

The reward for going through this process, as Scrooge did, is a true and lasting change in our financial thinking, choices and behaviors.

Rescripting

To help our clients start the process of becoming present and viewing life and their financial situations with more objectivity and clarity, we have them write variations of their money scripts. For example, let's take one of Ebenezer's most entrenched money scripts: "You can never have enough money."

Now, let's list as many variations on this money script that could be true:

- Is it true people could find themselves in a financial situation where there isn't enough money? Of course.
- Is it also true there are financial situations where there is enough money? Certainly.
- Is it true that sometimes we have more than enough money? Yes.
- Is it true that sometimes we have the perception that there is not enough money, when there actually is enough? Again, yes.
- Is it true there are some circumstances where you can have too much money? Indeed.

Could it be true that there were some situations in Scrooge's life when he simply didn't have enough money? Absolutely. When he was a child and young man, Scrooge lived in poverty. Moreover, it is reasonable to conclude that like every other human alive, Scrooge's resources were not bottomless. Certainly there were some things he couldn't afford.

Is it true that Scrooge had financial situations for which he had enough money? It would appear that he had more than enough capital to run his business and own his own home.

And, is it true that there were some financial circumstances for which Scrooge had more than enough money? Certainly. Although he lived an impoverished lifestyle, he had more than enough money to live more abundantly, as is evident by the changes he eventually makes.

So we can see that Scrooge's money script, "You can never have enough money," was not a good fit for every financial situation in his life.

Let's rescript a money script common to many people today, and perhaps one that Mrs. Cratchit, who viewed Scrooge as being particularly cruel, evil and sinister, may have held "The rich obtained their wealth dishonestly."

Is this money script true? Have wealthy people obtained their wealth dishonestly? Certainly, some wealthy people have done so.

- Have some people become wealthy simply by being in the right place at the right time? Absolutely. Lottery winners, for example.

- Have some people become wealthy because they have been willing to take risks that others have not been willing to take? Certainly. The acting and music fields are filled with people who risked everything to follow their talents and dreams.
- Are there poor people who are dishonest? Of course.

Obviously, there are people who fall into each of these descriptions. The money script "The rich obtained their wealth dishonestly" is only one possibility, yet some people treat it as if it is a universal truth. Again, trying to apply the same script to all situations is what causes problems. When a person stops living as though a money script is the complete truth and begins to see clearly how different truths exist, the original money script loses its power. It is no longer an absolute truth. Scrooge's original script, "You can never be happy if you are poor," went through a rescripting process as he became more open to seeing the exceptions to his previously hard and fast money script.

> **Problems arise when people treat**
> **money scripts as if they are always accurate—**
> **complete and totally true for every situation.**

Let's rescript one of the more popular money scripts from chapter one: "More money will make things better."

Again, we can begin to see that this is only a partial truth. Here are some other questions to consider:

- Can receiving more money enhance your quality of life?

- Can receiving more money destroy your quality of life?
- Can receiving more money better a portion of your life while destroying another portion?

Again, the answer to all three questions is yes, depending on the specific financial situation. Like Scrooge, discovering the variations to our money scripts can help us free ourselves from self-defeating beliefs.

Every money script can be modified to fit a variety of financial situations.

The Ghost of Christmas Present helps Scrooge modify his old money scripts with new information and understandings. The process of modifying our money scripts disrupts our distorted thinking, breaks our denial and helps us assimilate new information so that we can begin to change our behavior.

Exercise 6
MODIFYING MONEY SCRIPTS

Now that you know how it works, you can try rescripting one or more of your money scripts. Look at the money scripts you identified in the exercise at the end of chapter 1. Choose a money script you want to modify, then rework it to fit at least three different financial situations. You may need to try this a few times before you see all the options. The process is more dynamic when you ask another person or a group of people to help you see the variations. The more entrenched your script, the more difficult it will be for you to see any variation.

The following story is a powerful and touching example of how a willingness to look closely at a money script can result in a healing that involves far more than our relationship with money.

Sweet Little Girl

I had it all, or so it might seem to others. I was a partner in a successful multimillion-dollar corporation, fortunate enough to have a number of great friends and a job I loved and was very good at. I interacted daily with the powerful, rich and famous. I had my own home, as well as dogs that loved me. I was a strong, confident, independent, successful businesswoman operating in a traditionally man's world with a serious bite that I would use if anyone even thought of messing with me. In a few short years, I had amassed most of the things that were supposed to make a person happy and complete. Yet, something was missing.

One thing missing was an intimate relationship, though I was not at all as concerned about that as my friends were. I had decided long ago not to get mixed up in one of those. It required far too much energy and would distract from the really important thing, my career. Also, I certainly wouldn't want anything like my parents had, or the relationships that I saw my contemporaries having. I had pretty much decided that intimate relationships were just one more of the many frauds that were perpetrated on the unsophisticated and foolish.

A family of my own? Children? Forget it! Although I adored my nieces and nephews, they loved me, and I had a wonderful time with the children of my friends and colleagues, children of my own would be *way too* expensive.

The biggest problem I had, if you can imagine it, was that I had and made far more money than any other member of my family did. I felt guilty about that. One sibling was a drug addict, another was frequently in and out of jail, and my parents had never been prudent with their money and continued to live hand to mouth. Over the years I had tried a number of things to help my family, mostly by giving them money, but nothing ever changed. They were gradually getting worse, and I was never able to save for my own future. I was actually living in debt so I could honestly say, "I don't have any to give you" when they would ask.

I share most everything, personal and professional, with my business partner, and he had witnessed my struggles with my family over the years. In fact, he had some similar struggles of his own.

He suggested that I might talk to some people who had helped him. I had been impressed with the changes I had seen in his life and decided to meet with them. One thing led to another, and I ended up at a six-day workshop designed and facilitated by Ted and Brad Klontz and Rick Kahler. It was to be quite an experience.

During the workshop, one of the exercises was challenging old money scripts. These are unconscious, never challenged beliefs and half-truths about money that we all internalize and then forget are there. When it was my turn, I shared one of my money scripts with the group.

"Children are expensive," I said. I sat back in my chair, barely able to control the smugness that I felt. Surely, there could be no disputing that fact. Everyone knows that script is so true, it couldn't possibly be challenged.

My fellow group members did their best to provide me with variations on my script, but to be quite honest, their attempts were weak. As the time neared for ending the exercise, I was even more convinced that my "Children are expensive" ("and that's why I never want any!") script was unassailable.

Almost at the last moment, one of my fellow group members—a gentle, reserved English woman—looked me straight in the eye and said in a quiet voice, "Actually, children are priceless." She immediately followed up with, "Just like you were priceless as a little girl."

I reeled back in shock. It was like someone or something had reached into my soul and lovingly touched its most tender part—a place I had not visited in a very long time, if ever. You see, my mom had left me, my brother and my sister when I was five years old. I was told that she didn't love us any more or want to be around us.

What I have recently learned is that when traumatic things like that happen, little kids can't help but believe that somehow they are responsible. So, the story I made up was that my siblings and I were too much. We were too needy, too much responsibility, too much of an interference in the important work of life, too expensive, just too much of everything—that must have been the reason why mom left us.

Family members told me that on the day my mom left, I went into my room, locked it and didn't come out for five hours. They had to break the lock on my bedroom door to get to me.

As I sat through the remainder of the workshop, I began to realize that during that five hours that I had spent by myself in my bedroom at five years old, what was actually happening was that I had my first executive meeting with myself. During that meeting, I told that innocent five-year-old to stay there, to stay hidden if anyone came close. If they came too close, she was to bite them. She was to attack them before they had a chance to see her or get close. I also told that innocent child not to bother "me." I knew my brother, sister and I had to survive. Being the oldest, it was my job to see that that happened, and I couldn't do that with a whiney, needy kid-type hanging on.

During those five hours, I started building a concrete wall; eventually it would become so thick that no one could get through it, so tall that no one could get over it, so foreboding that people, if they even saw it, would shrink away in fear. I made it look like a monster lived there and from time to time, if anyone got too close, the monster would bite them. The entrance was so well disguised that for the next twenty-seven years I couldn't even find my way back in. When that little girl walked out of that room so many years before, she took with her the script that "kids are too expensive."

That might seem extreme, but that little girl needed that degree of protection. I grew up watching my sister and brother get emotionally, physically and sexually abused. I don't have any memories of that happening to me, but I do remember trying my whole childhood (and later as an adult) to help my siblings and protect them from what was happening. I wasn't successful at preventing bad things from happening to them, and I continued to carry my survivor shame and guilt about that. As an adult, part of my giving them money was an attempt to assuage that never-ending guilt.

Another one of the profound moments that I experienced during that workshop was an opportunity to search for the little girl that I had locked behind that wall so many years before. It would be a powerful reunion.

For reasons that I did not fully understand at the time, I had brought childhood photos of my sister and myself to the workshop. The therapeutic moment began for me when my counselor asked me to choose another group member to play the role of me as that five-year-old. Then the counselor asked me to look at the pictures and to respond to what I felt as I looked at them. The word that jumped out at me was how completely innocent those two small children looked. And as that word came to my mind and I looked at those two beautiful little girls standing there, I began sobbing. The counselor then directed me to look across the room at the person I had chosen to play me as that little girl and invited me to connect with her. As we began walking toward each other, our arms opened and we fell into each other's arms and began crying together.

My tears wouldn't stop as my body convulsed with the long-buried grief for that innocent little girl. It seemed for a moment that this grief, unleashed for the first time in almost thirty years, might go on forever. The therapist invited me to just hold this little girl in my arms. At the same time, someone playing the role of my mom held me. All three of us just cried, along with everyone else in the room—even the counselor.

The therapeutic moment closed with the therapist playing a song about understanding what it meant to love and be loved by another person. Unbelievably, the artist who sang that song was my business partner! As I lay there on the floor, gently crying, holding the person playing my five-year-old self and being held by someone, as my mother might have done had she been in my life, I felt a transformation, a shift deep inside of me.

During the following hours and days, it became clear to me that, God willing, I *do* want to have children, and I *do* want to have an intimate relationship. I was able to actually get a sense of what that might feel and look like. That was enough of a miracle, but there was to be more.

For my aftercare, it was suggested that I might want to nurture this newly restored relationship with myself. I had seen how perfectly beautiful and innocent I was then. I saw that that part of me was still alive. I also discovered that the people in the group seemed to truly love and treasure that part of me. I called her "my sweet little girl." I made a plan to get copies of the pictures that I have of me at age five and put one in my home and one in my office. I would look at one before I went to work and again at night just before I went to bed. I would look at the other on my desk at work, to remind me of my new commitment to love and honor that part of me.

The night the workshop was over I returned home. When I walked into my house, I found a strange, tall gift, complete with card, on my living room table. When I opened the gift (I always open my gifts first!), there, to my absolute awe, was an oil portrait of me at the age of five. It was taken from a photograph I had shown my business partner two years earlier. It was the most beautifully done portrait I had ever seen. The note read: "I had this painted in honor of the child you are healing. This sweet little girl reminds me of who you really are, and I celebrate her."

I couldn't believe it. How had he known what my experience at the workshop was going to be? How could he have known of my new commitment to display some pictures of me as a little girl? How could he have known about the exact name I had given myself? He had used the name in the card he had written days before my experience. Then I remembered: he is on the same journey, and that's how he knew what I might be experiencing. I could not stop crying for a very long time. Some might call it a coincidence; I choose to consider it my very own miracle.

To say the financial integration workshop was life changing would be an understatement. I went to the program scared about money, fearful of its grip on me and my interpersonal relationships, and not sure how to change my life. I left the program with the realization that it wasn't "money" I was having trouble with, but the thirty-four years of wounds, negative scripts and unidentified hidden treasures that were causing me pain and leaving me feeling secluded. I left the program a new woman.

Armed with a newfound sense of hope and power—and the exit plan I worked on during the last twenty-four hours of the program—I returned home and began creating a new map for what I wanted my life to look like. I was ready for real change. The great thing about all of this was that unlike any great "deals" I'd done in the past (which is my strong suit professionally), this would be the first time I would allow my inner child, my whole self, to be a part of a transaction. I would tackle all things head on with strength but also with tenderness.

The map I devised covered three primary areas: finance, interpersonal relationships and emotional growth. I have always done well when I have a plan, and this would prove to be my most important one yet.

In the finance category, I divided my goals into three phases: (1) to be free from my almost $30,000 of debt, (2) to aggressively begin executing my long-term retirement goals and (3) to work on diversifying my portfolio and building my personal wealth. In the nearly three and a half months since the program, I am two payments away from completing phase one, I have increased my 401k retirement investment to the maximum allowed by law and I am currently working on boosting the retirement savings elements of my portfolio. This process has been immensely freeing.

In the interpersonal relationships category, I desperately wanted to free myself from the guilt I had always carried about my professional success and the lack thereof in my family. I wanted to be free from thinking it wasn't okay for me to be successful, have money and a great life when my family was so lacking. In the past, this terrible feeling of guilt had caused me to give up my life savings twice, strive to be a savior for every and any problem, and sabotage my own happiness.

In my program work, I realized that I am not responsible for my family members' terrible misfortunes and poor choices, but I *am* responsible for my success and happiness. Since the workshop, I have discussed my goals with my family, set clear boundaries for myself and my interactions with them, and most important, given up my long-standing role as matriarch.

I have had two incidents test my strength in these months, both of which would have been considered my Achilles' heels in the past. I am proud to say that, though it wasn't easy, I stood strong through both. The first was my brother's call from prison. He was concerned that the money for his private attorney (which I had given him a year ago) had run out and that he might have to rely on a public defender. Instead of running to his rescue, I kindly told him that public defenders are there for those who do not have the means to hire privately (which he didn't), and that he should take full advantage of them. I encouraged him to work on preparing for his defense and promised my support by supplying books or any learning materials he might need to educate himself regarding this self-inflicted situation.

The second problem included a visit to my sister and her children who live on welfare and in a general state of disarray. I have never agreed with my sister's lifestyle. Despite countless opportunities, she has never made any real attempts to change and live responsibly. Typically, a visit would prompt me to try to help her see that there's a better way to live. I always left disappointed. After fifteen years of this type of judgment, negative interaction and pain, it was time for me to let it go.

Instead of falling back into my old role, I chose to just show her and her children love. I offered no suggestions for improvement and didn't even comment on the strange man walking around the house half-dressed. I just loved them. This was very hard. For the first time I witnessed my sister, my love, for who she is and decided to love her anyway. On my drive home I let years of pain and fear go with my tears. It was beautiful.

In the category of emotional growth, I decided my initial small steps would be to take more chances and live more authentically.

Though I have always been a strong woman, I have always been terrified of rejection, convinced I wasn't good enough for real love and affection. I was afraid to acknowledge my real feelings. They were always too real. Well, in the last fifteen weeks I have taken risks that make me blush, acknowledged my true feelings and honored them in ways that have made my friends and business partners shout with glee. And I am loving it!

For the first time in my adult life I am not carrying around constant anxiety and fear. I have been able to stop taking my anxiety medication because living authentically in the moment has taken away my need for scripting and overblown hypervigilance. I feel free.

The Motivation to Change

Just as the Ghost of Christmas Present is about to leave, he opens his cloak and shows Scrooge a vision of two small children. One is named "Want" and the other "Ignorance." The Spirit reminds Scrooge, and perhaps all of us, that of the two, "Ignorance" presents the greatest danger to his well-being. It's what we don't know that can hurt us.

After his visit with the Ghost of Christmas Present, Scrooge finally believes it is important for him to change and seems confident he can change. But is he ready?

There is still an important step missing: a glimpse at the consequences of his continued actions. Scrooge can't yet see the consequences of continuing in his current life path. He has heard what others think of him. He can finally see what "normal" is and regrets some of his past behavior. Still, does he really have the understanding he needs to make a meaningful and lasting change in his life? Dickens thinks not.

That motivation comes from his next visitor, the Ghost of Christmas Future. This spirit silently paints a vivid picture of the future that Scrooge will face if he doesn't change. For many of us, this pain is the tool that inspires change. If we are lucky enough, we get to experience it while we still have time to alter things. Once more, Scrooge is about to experience the pain that brings about transformation.

Applying the Wisdom of This Chapter

Who are you? Who do others say that you are?

1. Write down five adjectives or descriptive phrases that you would use to describe yourself.

2. Next, ask the five (or ten, or fifteen if you are really feeling brave) people closest to you to list five adjectives they would use to describe you to someone else. You might ask them this question: "If you were talking to a friend of yours who didn't know me and you were talking about me, what five words or phrases would you use to describe who I am?"

3. Examine differences and similarities between the two lists. It is common for those who do this type of exercise to be surprised—even shocked—by the differences in their perception of themselves and how they are seen by others, both in positive and negative ways.

4. Write down any areas where your core values are not in line with your behaviors.

5

THE LAST OF THE THREE SPIRITS—

STAGE FOUR: CONTEMPLATING THE FUTURE

*It's good to have an end
to the journey, but it's the journey
that matters in the end.*

—URSULA K. LEGUIN

"Lead on! Lead on! The night is waning fast, and it is precious time to me. Lead on, Spirit."

—Scrooge to the Ghost of Christmas
Future, *A Christmas Carol*

People once believed that ghosts could foretell the future, including death. Thus, it came as no surprise to Victorian readers that the Ghost of Christmas Future—a hooded specter dressed in black—is Death. The spirit would eventually lead Scrooge to see his own death and Tiny Tim's death.

Scrooge feared this ghost more than either of the previous visitors. By this point in the story, however, Scrooge is actually excited by the thought of what the Ghost of Christmas Future might show him. Without a single word, the spirit takes Scrooge to a man's deathbed. It illuminates this miserable person's death, showing that no one cared or mourned for him. The cleaning woman steals his clothing and bed curtains. Even a man who owes a debt to the deceased feels a guilty joy that he might have a few more days before his debt is due.

Amazingly, Scrooge does not realize that the dead man is himself. Scrooge overhears conversations about the corpse. He sees a dead body in his own chamber covered by a sheet. The ghost gestures for him to pull back the sheet, but Scrooge refuses. Finally, Scrooge is led to his own bare grave to read his name on the headstone. Enlightenment arrives like a thunder-clap, shattering the last remnants of Scrooge's denial. He sees the legacy he will leave behind and he doesn't like it:

> *"Am I that man who lay upon the bed?" Scrooge cried,*
> *upon his knees. "Spirit! Hear me! I am not the man I was.*
> *I will honor Christmas in my heart and keep it all the year."*

We see similar reactions from many of our clients. It's as if they have been gathering bits and pieces of their lives together when suddenly, in a flash of realization, all those bits merge together. The desire to change and the knowledge about what to change come together, resulting in a flash of insight: the consequences of not changing are clear, but, even better, so are the possibilities and opportunities that come *with* change.

We want to point out that had Scrooge started with his future, he would not have had the clarity to really see it. It was only because Scrooge had visited his past and present, in that order, that he was able and ready to see his future.

By looking into the future, we can see the consequences of our continued actions. Often, these consequences can be catastrophic, and this awareness creates the motivation to change.

PRINCIPLE #4: AWARENESS OF CONSEQUENCES CREATES MOTIVATION

This is exactly what happens to Scrooge. When he sees the future—that is, when he *really* sees the consequences of his actions—he is immediately distraught. The future is so horrific that he begs for a second chance. He fervently desires to prevent that future from occurring at all costs.

A SECOND CHANCE

A popular story claims that in 1888 a man by the name of Alfred picked up the morning newspaper and was shocked when he saw his own name in the headlines. Alfred was a famous inventor, and the newspapers had mistakenly published the story of his death, when in fact his brother Ludwig had been the one to die the day before.

Much to Alfred's chagrin, his most famous invention, which he had originally developed to aid excavation, had been converted to use as a horrific weapon of war. Even when his invention was originally contemplated for as a weapon, he reasoned that the weapon's potential for causing massive death and destruction was so obvious that it would never be used for such a purpose. Unfortunately, that wasn't the case.

On that morning in 1888, French headlines screamed, "The Merchant of Death is Dead!" That was how the world would view his entire life! That would be his eternal legacy. Shaken, Alfred clearly saw the consequences of his actions. He resolved to change how he would be remembered.

In his will, Alfred left his enormous wealth to fund "prizes to those who, during the preceding year, shall have conferred the greatest benefit on mankind." The prizes to be awarded were in the fields of chemistry, physics, medicine, literature and, ironically, peace.

Alfred, like Scrooge, had seen the consequences of his actions and made a conscious decision to do everything possible to change his legacy.

Today, Alfred Nobel, once seen as the Merchant of Death, is remembered not as much for his invention of dynamite, which is but a footnote in history, but rather for his creation of the yearly prizes, the most famous of which is the Nobel Peace Prize.

Scrooge's New Legacy

All around us, we see the effects of other people's destructive money scripts. They imprison, wound, paralyze and destroy. Even so, it is often difficult to see the destructive effects of our own money scripts.

Once Scrooge recognized the consequences of his miserly behaviors, he resolved to change. From that moment on, the character that everyone typically envisions when they think of Scrooge—the coldhearted, miserly skinflint—was gone.

**No matter how far you have gone on
the wrong road, turn back.**

—Turkish Proverb

In a way, the old Scrooge was metaphorically dead. Arising from the ashes was the new Scrooge. Confident that he could change at least parts of the future, Scrooge resolved to do good wherever and whenever he could.

How to Anticipate Consequences

We've established that being aware of the consequences of our actions can create motivation for change. But how do we know what the consequences of our actions will be? After all, you may be wondering, how can you predict the future?

This is where the help and guidance of a professional can be most useful. Scrooge would not have seen his future without the guidance of the Ghost of Christmas Future. You will remember that this final ghost didn't speak. He simply, yet effectively, guided Scrooge from scene to scene. With that help, Scrooge did the rest of the work. He "got it" without the specter speaking one word.

Today, our guides to the future take the form of therapists, coaches, attorneys, accountants and financial planners. Effective ones have the expertise to look at our current situation and show us the future possibilities if we continue to walk the same path.

If we have done our work with our past and present, it won't take much effort for us to see and understand the consequences of our current financial behaviors and be motivated to change.

Once motivation to change is established, the transformation is almost complete. It simply takes action.

Manny is typical of our clients who, having visited their past and present, want to take a clear look at their future. In Manny's case, this was a retirement projection. We started the session by posting on a wall his current situation. The situation was not pretty and included the age at which his money would run out at his current rate of spending. This forty-five-year-old man wanted to retire at age fifty-five, but actually would be out of money by age fifty-eight if he continued his current behaviors. We shared with him three options that could give him enough money to last his lifetime. These options assumed various levels of spending cuts and retirement income. This new knowledge motivated Manny to reduce his spending by 40 percent within a year, something his advisors had been trying to get him to do for more than ten years.

What is your future if you don't change your current behaviors surrounding money?

Will *you* change?

To help you become more acutely aware of what is vitally important to you, we would like you to do the exercise in the box following.

**There is always time to make
right what is wrong.**

—Susan Griffin

Applying the Wisdom of This Chapter

Brainstorm a list of all the things that you would regret or feel badly about not having done if your life were to end tomorrow. Include everything you can see yourself regretting, including any unfinished business in your most important relationships, things you wish you had said to loved ones, things you feel about your loved ones that you hope they know, places you wish you had visited, adventures you wish you had undertaken, things you wish you had learned, etc.

From this simple, yet often profound list, you may get some very significant clues as to what things are important for you to accomplish to live your life with greater passion, meaning and integrity—as Scrooge did!

6

A New Script—

Stage Five: Transformation and Action

Things do not change,
we do.

—Henry David Thoreau, *Walden*

"I will live in the Past, Present, and Future!
The Spirits of all Three
shall reside in me."

—Scrooge, *A Christmas Carol*

After the horrific vision of the future, Scrooge awakens in his own bedroom on Christmas Day to the wonderful knowledge that the terrible events foretold by the Ghost of Christmas Future have not yet happened. There is still time.

With a rush of emotion, Scrooge realizes that for the first time since he was a small child his senses are alive. Through his experiences with the ghosts, he became aware and felt his long-repressed feelings. The difficult feelings of fear, anger, mistrust and sadness have been replaced by lighter feelings of peace and happiness. He has a clarity that is beyond anything he's ever experienced. His outsides and insides are in harmony; he is experiencing what we call integrity. He sees the possibilities for abundance everywhere. Recognizing that the dismal future he has seen can still be prevented, Scrooge is overcome with joy:

"'I am as happy as an angel, I am as merry as a schoolboy. . . .' Running to the window, he opened it and put out his head. No fog, no mist; clear, bright, jovial, stirring; Golden sunlight; Heavenly sky; sweet fresh air; merry bells. Oh, glorious. Glorious!"

It is the same world that existed the day before; Scrooge just sees it differently.

Scrooge's enlightenment was complete. Dickens writes:

"Scrooge was better than his word. He did it all and infinitely more; and to Tiny Tim, who did NOT die, he was a second father. He became as good a friend, as good a master, and as good a man as the good old city knew, or any other good old city, town, or borough in the good old world. Some people laughed to see the alteration in him; but his own heart laughed, and that was quite enough for him."

Scrooge's awakening has progressed through five distinct stages, until he is transformed into a new person. We can see these stages in each chapter of *A Christmas Carol.*

1. **Denial and Intervention.** Scrooge resists three well-wishers. "Bah! Humbug!" He learns that his beliefs drive his behaviors. Marley's ghost intervenes, helping Scrooge to hit bottom and become aware of his need to change. He fears the process and attempts to bargain with Marley's ghost. He learns that *denial inhibits change.*
2. **Exploring the Past.** Scrooge is reluctant to go into his past. He views the traumatic events that formed his beliefs about money. He learns that *to heal you must feel.*

He fully feels the repressed emotions associated with those events. Finally, he struggles with the Ghost of Christmas Past to repress the past.

3. **Understanding the Present.** Having awakened to his hidden feelings and once dulled senses, Scrooge gains awareness of reality with the Ghost of Christmas Present. As a result, he learns that *it pays to be present,* and that he can live in more abundance, authenticity and clarity.

4. **Contemplating the Future.** The Ghost of Christmas Future helps Scrooge see the consequences of his old behaviors, and this *awareness creates motivation.* Scrooge begs to be given a second chance to change. He promises, "I will honor Christmas in my heart, and try to keep it all the year."

5. **Transformation and Action.** Finally, Scrooge changes his behavior. He learns that *transformation requires action* and he becomes "as good a friend, as good a master, and as good a man as the good city knew."

PRINCIPLE #5: TRANSFORMATION REQUIRES ACTION

The Power to Change

In the closing paragraphs of *A Christmas Carol,* Dickens makes it clear that Scrooge took action and found the power to change. It wasn't a temporary change, a change that might come for a few days, weeks or months through the power of